CAMBRIDGE LIBRARY COLLECTION

Books of enduring scholarly value

History

The books reissued in this series include accounts of historical events and movements by eye-witnesses and contemporaries, as well as landmark studies that assembled significant source materials or developed new historiographical methods. The series includes work in social, political and military history on a wide range of periods and regions, giving modern scholars ready access to influential publications of the past.

Journal

Frances Anne Kemble (1809–1893) was a famous London-born actress who toured the United States with her father for several years before marrying the Philadelphia land-owner and heir Pierce Butler. Her two-volume journal, first published in 1835 under her married name, shocked the American public for its ungenerous and often biting criticisms of the young country. Detailing Kemble's voyage to and tour of the United States, the journal contains first-hand accounts of the cities of the eastern seaboard in the early nineteenth-century and the manners and customs of its people. Noted for its candid observations and strong personal style, Kemble's journal remains one of her most lasting literary works.

Cambridge University Press has long been a pioneer in the reissuing of out-of-print titles from its own backlist, producing digital reprints of books that are still sought after by scholars and students but could not be reprinted economically using traditional technology. The Cambridge Library Collection extends this activity to a wider range of books which are still of importance to researchers and professionals, either for the source material they contain, or as landmarks in the history of their academic discipline.

Drawing from the world-renowned collections in the Cambridge University Library, and guided by the advice of experts in each subject area, Cambridge University Press is using state-of-the-art scanning machines in its own Printing House to capture the content of each book selected for inclusion. The files are processed to give a consistently clear, crisp image, and the books finished to the high quality standard for which the Press is recognised around the world. The latest print-on-demand technology ensures that the books will remain available indefinitely, and that orders for single or multiple copies can quickly be supplied.

The Cambridge Library Collection will bring back to life books of enduring scholarly value (including out-of-copyright works originally issued by other publishers) across a wide range of disciplines in the humanities and social sciences and in science and technology.

Journal

VOLUME 1

FANNY KEMBLE

CAMBRIDGE
UNIVERSITY PRESS

CAMBRIDGE UNIVERSITY PRESS

Cambridge, New York, Melbourne, Madrid, Cape Town, Singapore,
São Paolo, Delhi, Dubai, Tokyo

Published in the United States of America by Cambridge University Press, New York

www.cambridge.org
Information on this title: www.cambridge.org/9781108003919

© in this compilation Cambridge University Press 2009

This edition first published 1835
This digitally printed version 2009

ISBN 978-1-108-00391-9 Paperback

JOURNAL

BY

FRANCES ANNE BUTLER.

IN TWO VOLUMES.

VOL. I.

LONDON:
JOHN MURRAY, ALBEMARLE STREET.
MDCCCXXXV.

PREFACE.

A PREFACE appears to me necessary to
this book, in order that the expectation
with which the English reader might open
it should not be disappointed.

Some curiosity has of late been excited
in England with regard to America: its
political existence is a momentous experiment, upon which many eyes are fixed, in
anxious watching of the result; and such
accounts as have been published of the
customs and manners of its societies, and
the natural wonders and beauties of its
scenery, have been received and read with
considerable interest in Europe. This
being the case, I should be loth to present these volumes to the English public
without disclaiming both the intention and
the capability of adding the slightest detail

of any interest to those which other travellers have already furnished upon these subjects.

This book is, what it professes to be, my personal journal, and not a history or a description of men and manners in the United States.

Engaged in an arduous profession, and travelling from city to city in its exercise, my leisure, and my opportunities, would have been alike inadequate to such a task. The portion of America which I have visited has been a very small one, and, I imagine, by no means that from which the most interesting details are to be drawn. I have been neither to the south nor to the west; consequently have had no opportunity of seeing two large portions of the population of this country, — the enterprising explorers of the late wildernesses on the shores of the Mississippi, — and the black race of the slave states, both classes of men presenting peculiarities of infinite interest to the traveller: the one, a source of energy and growing strength, the other, of disease and decay, in this vast political body.

My sphere of observation has been confined to the Atlantic cities, whose astonishing mercantile prosperity, and motley mongrel societies, though curious under many aspects, are interesting but under few.

What I registered were my immediate impressions of what I saw and heard; of course, liable to all the errors attendant upon first perceptions, and want of time and occasion for maturer investigation. The notes I have added while preparing the text for the press; and such opinions and details as they contain are the result of a longer residence in this country, and a somewhat better acquaintance with the people of it.

Written, as my journal was, day by day, and often after the fatigues of a laborious evening's duty at the theatre, it has infinite sins of carelessness to answer for; and but that it would have taken less time and trouble to re-write the whole book, or rather write a better, I would have endeavoured to correct them, — though, indeed, I was something of Alfieri's mind about it: — " Quanto poi allo stile, io penso di lasciar fare alla penna, e di pochissimo lasciarlo scostarsi da quella triviale e spontanea naturalezza, con cui ho scritto quest' opera, dettata dal cuore e non dall' ingegno ; e che sola può convenire a così umile tema."

However, my purpose is not to write an apology for my book, or its defects, but simply to warn the English reader, before he is betrayed into its perusal, that it is a purely egotistical record, and by no means a history of America.

JOURNAL.

Wednesday, August 1st, 1832.

ANOTHER break in my journal, and here I am on board the Pacific, bound for America, having left home, and all the world behind. — Well ! *

 * * * * *

We reached the quay just as the ship was being pulled, and pushed, and levered to the entrance of the dock; — the quays were lined with people, among them were several known faces, — Mr. ——, Mr. ——. M—— came on board to take my letters, and bid me good-by. * *

 * * * * *

I had a bunch of carnations in my hand, which I had snatched from our drawing-room chimney; — English flowers ! —dear English flowers ! they will be withered long before I again see land, but I will keep them until I once more stand upon the soil on which they grew. * *

 * * * * *

VOL. I.   B

The sky had become clouded, and the wind blew cold.   *   *   *

 *   *   *   *   *

Came down and put our narrow room to rights.

 *   *   *   *   *

Worked at my Bible cover till dinner time. We dined at half-past three. — The table was excellent — cold dinner, because it was the first day — but every thing was good; and champagne, and dessert, and every luxury imaginable, rendered it as little like a ship-dinner as might be. The man who sat by me was an American; very good-natured, and talkative. Our passengers are all men, with the exception of three; a nice, pretty-looking girl, who is going out with her brother; a fat old woman, and a fat young one. I cried almost the whole of dinner-time.   *   *

 *   *   *   *   *

After dinner the ladies adjourned to their own cabin, and the gentlemen began to debate about regulating the meal hours. They adopted the debating society tone, called my poor dear father to the chair, and presently I heard, oh horror! (what I had not thought to hear again for six weeks,) the clapping of hands. They sent him in to consult us about the dinner-hour: and we having decided four o'clock, the debate continued with considerable merriment. Presently my father, Colonel ——, and Mr. ——, came into our cabin:—the former read us Washington Irving's speech at the New York dinner. Some of it is very beautiful, all of it is in good feeling—it made me cry. Oh my home, my land, England, glorious little England! from which this bragging big baby was born, how my heart yearns towards your earth! I sat working till the gentlemen left us, and then wrote journal.   *   *

  *   *   *   *   *

I am weary and sad, and will try to go and sleep.—It rains: I cannot see the moon.

Thursday, 2d.

It rained all night, and in the morning the wind had died away, and we lay rocking, becalmed on the waveless waters. At eight o'clock they brought me some breakfast, after which I got up; while dressing, I could not help being amused at hearing the cocks crowing, and the cow lowing, and geese and ducks gabbling, as though we were in the midst of a farm-yard. At half-past ten, having finished my toilet, I emerged; and Miss —— and I walked upon deck. The sea lay still, and grey, without ridge or sparkle, a sheet of lead; the sky was of the same dull colour. The deck was wet and comfortless. We were but just off Holyhead: two or three ships stood against the horizon, still as ourselves. The whole was melancholy:—and sadder than all, sat a poor woman, dressed in mourning, in a corner of the deck; she was a steerage passenger, and I never saw so much sorrow in any face. Poor thing! poor thing! was her heart aching for home, and kindred left behind her? It made mine ach to look at her. We walked up and down for an hour. I like my companion well; she is a nice, young quiet thing, just come from a country home. Came down, and began getting out books for my German lesson, but turning rather awful, left my learning on the floor, and betook myself to my berth. Slept nearly till dinner time. At dinner I took my place at table, but presently the misery returned; and getting up, while I had sufficient steadiness left to walk becomingly down the room, I came to my cabin; my dinner followed me thither, and, lying on my back, I very comfortably discussed it. Got up, devoured some raspberry tart, and grapes, and being altogether delightful again, sat working and singing till tea-time: after which, wrote journal, and now to bed. How strange it seems to hear these Americans speaking in English of *the English !* — " Oh, hame, hame, hame wad I be," — but it is not time to sing that yet.

Friday, 3d.

Breakfasted at eight; got up, and dressed, and came upon deck. The day was lovely, the sea one deep dark sapphire, the sky bright and cloudless, the wind mild and soft, too mild to fill our sails, which hung lazily against the masts, — but enough to refresh the warm summer's sky, and temper the bright sun of August that shone above us. Walked upon deck with Miss —— and Captain Whaite: the latter is a very intelligent, good-natured person; rough and bluff, and only seven and twenty; which makes his having the command of a ship rather an awful consideration. At half-past eleven got my German, and worked at it till half-past one, then got my work; and presently we were summoned on deck by sound of bell, and oyes! oyes! oyes! — and a society was established for the good demeanour and sociability of the passengers. My father was in the chair. Mr. —— was voted secretary, Dr. —— attorney-general;

a badge was established, rules and regulations laid down, a code framed, and much laughing and merriment thence ensued. Worked till dinner-time. After dinner, went on deck, took a brisk walk for half an hour with Captain Whaite. Established myself to work, and presently we were all summoned to attend a mock trial of Colonel ——, which made us all laugh most exceedingly. We adopted titles — I chose my family appellation of Puddledock: many of the names were very absurd, and as a penalty ensued upon not giving every body their proper designation, much amusement arose from it. When the trial was over, we played at dumb crambo, and earth, air, and water, with infinite zeal, till tea-time. After tea, we were summoned on deck to see the ship make a tack. The wind was against us, the sea inky black, the pale clear moon stood high against the sail—presently, with a whooping and yaw-awling that mocks description, the fair ship was turned away from the wind, the sails veered round, and she set in another course. We remained on deck, the gentlemen gathered round us, and singing began: — it went round and round by turns, some of our voices were very sweet, and, upon the whole, 't was time pleasantly spent. Came to bed at ten.

Wednesday, 15th.

Here's a lapse! thanks to head winds, a rolling sea, and their result, sickness, sadness, sorrow. I've been better for the last two days, thank God! and take to my book again. Rose at eight, dawdled about, and then came up stairs. Breakfasted, sat working at my Bible cover till lunchtime. — Somebody asked me if I had any of Mrs. Siddons's hair; I sent for my dressing-box, and forthwith it was overhauled, to use the appropriate phrase, by half the company, whom a rainy day had reduced to a state of worse than usual want of occupation. The rain continued all day; we ladies dined in the round-house, the room down stairs being too close. The Captain and Colonel —— joined us afterwards, and began drinking champagne, and induced us to do the same. As evening came on, the whole of the passengers collected in the round-house. Mr. ——, Mr. D——, and I wrote a rhapsody; afterwards they fell to singing; while they did so, the sky darkened tremendously, the rain came pelting down, the black sea swelled, and rose, and broke upon the ship's sides into boiling furrows of foam, that fled like ghosts along the inky face of the ocean. The

ship scudded before the blast, and we managed to
keep ourselves warm by singing. After tea, for the
first time since I have been on board, got hold of
a pack of cards, (oh me, that it ever should come
to this !) and initiated Miss —— in the mysteries
of the intellectual game. Mercy ! how my home
rose before me as I did so. Played till I was tired;
dozed, and finally came to bed. Bed ! quotha !
't is a frightful misapplication of terms. Oh for a
bed ! a real bed; any manner of bed, but a bed
on shipboard ! And yet I have seen some fair
things : I have seen a universe of air and water;
I have seen the glorious sun come and look down
upon this rolling sapphire; I have seen the moon
throw her silver columns along the watery waste;
I have seen one lonely ship in her silent walk
across this wilderness, meet another, greet her,
and pass her, like a dream, on the wide deep;
I have seen the dark world of waters at midnight
open its mysterious mantle beneath our ship's prow,
and show below another dazzling world of light. I
have seen, what I would not but have seen, though
I have left my very soul behind me. England,
dear, dear England ! oh, for a handful of your
earth !

Thursday, 16*th.*

Another day, another day! the old fellow posts as well over water as over land! Rose at about half-past eight, went up to the round-house; breakfasted, and worked at my Bible cover. As soon as our tent was spread, went out on deck: took a longish walk with Mr.———. I like him very much; his face would enchant Lavater, and his skull ecstacise the Combes. Lay down under our rough pavilion, and heard the gentlemen descant very learnedly upon freemasonry. A book called " Adventures of an Irish Gentleman," suggested the conversation; in which are detailed, some of the initiatory ceremonies, which appear to me so incredibly foolish, that I can scarce believe them, even making mankind a handsome allowance for absurdity. I soon perceived that the discussion was likely to prove a serious one, for in America, it seems, 'tis made a political question; and our Boston friend, and the Jacksonite, fell to rather sharply about it. The temperance of the former, however, by retreating from the field, spared us further argumentation. One thing I marvel at:— are the institutions of men stronger to bind men, than those of God; and does masonry effect good, which Christianity does not? — a silly query, by the way; for doubtless men act the good, but forbear to act the evil, before each other's eyes; which they think nothing of doing, or leaving undone, under those of God.

Gossiped till lunch-time; afterwards took up Childe Harold, — commend me to that! I thought of dear H———. She admires Byron more than I do; and yet how wildly I did, how deeply I do still, worship his might, majesty, and loveliness. We dined up stairs, and after dinner, I and Mr. ——— took a long walk on deck; talking flimsy morality, and philosophy; the text of which were generalities, but all the points individualities: I was amused in my heart at him and myself. He'd a good miss of me at ———: heaven knows, I was odious enough! and therein his informer was right. The day was bright, and bitter cold, — the sea blue, and transparent as that loveliest line in Dante,

"Dolce color di oriental zaffiro,"

with a lining of pearly foam, and glittering spray, that enchanted me. Came and sat down again : — wrote doggerel for the captain's album, about the captain's ship, which, when once I am out of her,

I'll swear I love infinitely. Read aloud to them some of Byron's short poems, and that glorious hymn to the sea, in Childe Harold:—mercy, how fine it is! Lay under our canvass shed till nine o'clock: — the stars were brilliant in the intense blue sky, the wind had dropped, the ship lay still — we sang a song or two, supped, and came in; where, after inditing two rhapsodies, we came to bed.

Friday, 17*th.*

On my back all day : mercy, how it ached too! the ship reeled about like a drunken thing. I lay down and began reading Byron's life. As far as I have gone (which is to his leaving England) there is nothing in it but what I expected to find, — the fairly sown seeds of the after-harvest he bore. Had he been less of an egotist, would he have been so great a poet?— I question it. His fury and wrath at the severe injustice of his critics reminds me, by the by, of those few lines in the Athenæum, which I read the other day, about poetical shoemakers, dairy-maids, plough-men, and myself. After all, what matters it?— " If this thing be of God," the devil can't overthrow it; if it be not, why the printer's devil may. What

can it signify what is said? If truth be truth to the
end of reckoning, why, that share of her, if any,
which I possess, must endure when recorded as
long as truth endures. I almost wonder Byron
was moved by criticism : I should have thought
him at once too highly armed, and too self-wrap-
ped, to care for it; — however, if a wasp's sting
have such virtue in it, 'tis as well it should have
been felt as keenly as it was. — Ate nothing but
figs and raisins; in the evening some of our gentlemen came into our cabin, and sat with us; I,
in very desperation and sea-sickness, began embroidering one of my old nightcaps, wherein I
persevered till sleep overtook me.

Saturday, 18th.

Rose at about half-past eight, dawdled about
as usual, breakfasted in the round-house — by
the by, before I got out of bed, read a few
more pages of Byron's life. I don't exactly
understand the species of sentimental *galimatias*
Moore talks about Byron's writing with the same
penfull of ink, " Adieu, adieu, my native land!"
and "Hurra! Hodgson, we are going." It proves
nothing except what I firmly believe, that we must
not look for the real feelings of writers in their

works — or rather, that what they give us, and what we take for heart feeling, is head weaving — a species of emotion engendered somewhere betwixt the bosom and the brain, and bearing the same proportion of resemblance to reality that a picture does; that is — like feeling, but not feeling — like sadness, but not sadness — like what it appears, but not indeed that very thing : and the greater a man's power of thus producing *sham realities*, the greater his main qualification for being a poet. —After breakfast, sat like Lady Alice in the old song, embroidering my midnight coif. Got Colonel —— to read Quentin Durward to us as we sat working under our canvass pavilion.

* * * * *

Our company consists chiefly of traders in cloth and hardware, clerks, and counting-house men — a species with but few peculiarities of interest to me, who cannot talk pounds, shillings, and pence, as glibly as less substantial trash. Most of them have crossed this trifling ditch half a dozen times in their various avocations. But though they belong to the same sort generally, they differ enough individually for the amusement of observation. That poor widower, whose remarks on the starry inside of the sea attracted my attention the other evening, put into my hands to-day a couple of pretty little books enough; a sort of hotch-potch, or to speak more sweetly, pot-pourri praise of women—passages selected from various authors who have done us the honour to remember us in their good commendations. There were one or two most eloquent and exquisite passages from Jeremy Taylor—one on love that enchanted me. I should like to copy it. What a contrast to that exquisite thing of Shelley's, "What is Love?" and yet they are both beautiful, powerful, and true. I could have helped them to sundry more passages on this subject, particularly from my oracle. Mr. —— read to us after lunch, and we sat very happily under our *yawning* till the rain drove us in. No wind, the sea one rippleless sheet of lead, and the sky just such another. Our main-top gallant-mast had been split in one of our late blows, and I went out in the rain to see them restore the spar. Towards evening the wind faired and freshened, in consequence of which, our gentlemen's spirits rose; and presently, in spite of the rain, they were dancing, singing, and romping like mad things on the quarter-deck. It was Saturday —holiday on board ship—the men were all dismissed to their grog. Mr. —— and I sang through a whole volume of Moore's melodies; and at ten o'clock (for the first time since our second day on board) we of the petticoats adjourned to the gentlemen's cabin to drink "sweethearts and wives," according to the approved sailors' practice. It made me sad to hear them, as they lifted their glasses to their lips, pass round the toast, "Sweethearts and wives!" I drank in my heart — "Home and dear H——." One thing amused me a good deal : — the Captain proposed as a toast, "The Ladies — God bless them," which accordingly was being duly drunk when I heard, close to my elbow, a devout, half audible — "and the Lord deliver us!" This from a man with a face like one of Retsch's most grotesque etchings, and an expression half humorous, half terrified, sent me into fits of laughter. They sang a song or two, and at twelve we left them to their meditations, which presently reached our ears in the sound, not shape, of "Health to Bacchus," in full chorus, to which tune I said my prayers.

Sunday, 19th.

Did not rise till late — dressed and came on deck. The morning was brilliant; the sea, bold, bright, dashing its snowy crests against our ship's sides, and flinging up a cloud of glittering spray round the prow. I breakfasted — and then amused

myself with finding the lessons, collects, and psalms
for the whole ship's company. After lunch, they
spread our tent, a chair was placed for my father,
and the little bell being rung, we collected in our
rude church. It affected me much, this praying on
the lonely sea, in the words that at the same hour
were being uttered by millions of kindred tongues
in our dear home. There was something, too,
impressive and touching in this momentary union
of strangers, met but for a passing day, to part perhaps never to behold each other's faces again, in
the holiest of all unions, that of Christian worship.
Here I felt how close, how strong that wondrous tie of common faith that thus gathered our
company, unknown and unconnected by any one
worldly interest or bond, to utter the same words
of praise and supplication, to think perhaps the
same thoughts of humble and trustful dependence
on God's great goodness in this our pilgrimage to
foreign lands, to yearn perhaps with the same
affection and earnest imploring of blessings towards
our native soil and its beloved ones left behind. —
Oh, how I felt all this as we spoke aloud that touching invocation, which is always one of my most
earnest prayers, "Almighty God, who hast promised when two or three are gathered together
in thy name," &c.   *   *   *   The bright cloudless

sky and glorious sea seemed to respond, in their silent magnificence, to our *Te Deum.*—I felt more of the excitement of prayer than I have known for many a day, and 't was good—oh ! very, very good !   *   *   *   *
    *   *   *   *   *

' Tis good to behold this new universe, this mighty sea which he hath made, this glorious cloud-less sky, where hang, like dew drops, his scattered worlds of light—to see all this and say,—

" These are thy glorious works, parent of good ! "

After prayers, wrote journal. Some sea weed floated by the ship to-day, borne from the gulf stream; I longed to have it, for it told of land : gulls too came wheeling about, and the little pet-terels like sea-swallows skimmed round and round, now resting on the still bosom of the sunny sea, now flickering away in rapid circles like black butterflies. They got a gun, to my horror, and wasted a deal of time in trying to shoot these feathered mariners; but they did not even succeed in scaring them. We went and sat on the forecastle to see the sun set : he did not go down cloudless, but dusky ridges of vapour stretched into ruddy streaks along the horizon, as his disk dipped into

the burnished sea.   The foam round the prow,
as the ship made way with all sail set before a
fair wind, was the most lovely thing I ever saw.
Purity, strength, glee, and wondrous beauty were
in those showers of snowy spray that sprang up
above the black ship's sides, and fell like a cataract
of rubies under the red sunlight.   We sat there
till evening came down; the sea, from brilliant
azure grew black as unknown things, the wind
freshened, and we left our cold stand to walk, or
rather run, up and down the deck to warm ourselves.   This we continued till, one by one, the
stars had lit their lamps in heaven: their wondrous brilliancy, together with the Aurora Borea-
lis, which rushed like sheeted ghosts along the sky,
and the stream of fire that shone round the ship's
way, made heaven and sea appear like one vast
world of flame, as though the thin blue veil of
air and the dark curtain of the waters were but
drawn across a universe of light.   Mercy, how
strange it was!   We stood at the stern, watching
the milky wake the ship left as she stole through
the eddying waters.   Came back to our gipsy en-
campment, where, by the light of a lantern, we
supped and sang sundry scraps of old songs.   At
ten came to bed.   *   *   *   *   *
    *   *   *   *   *

Took an observation of the sun's altitude at noon, and saw them hoist a main-top-royal sail, which looked very pretty as it was unreefed against the clear sky.

Monday, 20*th*.

Calm — utter calm — a roasting August sun, a waveless sea, the sails flapping idly against the mast, and our black cradle rocking to and fro without progressing a step. They lowered the boat, and went out rowing — I wanted to go, but they would not let me! A brig was standing some four miles off us, which, by the by, I was the first to see, except our mate, in my morning watch, which began at five o'clock, when I saw the moon set and the sun rise, and feel more than ever convinced that absolute reality is away from the purpose of works of art. The sky this morning was as like the sea-shore as ever sand and shingle were, the clouds lying along the horizon in pale dusky yellow layers, and higher up, floating in light brown ribbed masses, like the sands which grow wrinkled under the eternal smiling of the sea. Against the dim horizon, which blended with the violet-coloured sky, the mate then showed me, through the glass, the brig standing on the sea's edge, for all the world like one of the tiny birds who were wheeling and chirping round our ship's stern. I have done more in the shape of work to-day than any since the two first I spent on board; translated a German fable without much trouble, read a canto in Dante, ending with a valuation of fame. " O spirito gentil !" how lived fair wisdom in your soul — how shines she in your lays ! — Wrote journal, walked about, worked at my cap, in the evening danced merrily enough, quadrilles, country dances, La Boulangére, and the monaco ; fairly danced myself tired. Came to bed. But oh ! not to sleep — mercy, what a night ! The wind blowing like mad, the sea rolling, the ship pitching, bouncing, shuddering, and reeling, like a thing possessed. I lay awake, listening to her creaking and groaning, till two o'clock, when, sick of my sleepless berth, I got up and was going up stairs, to see, at least, how near drowning we were, when D ——, who was lying awake too, implored me to lie down again. I did so for the hundred and eleventh time, complaining bitterly that I should be stuffed down in a loathsome berth, cabined, cribbed, confined, while the sea was boiling below, and the wind bellowing above us. Lay till daylight, the gale increasing furiously; boxes, chairs, beds, and their contents, wooden valuables, and human invaluables, rolling about and clinging to one another in glorious confusion. At about eight o'clock, a tremendous sea took the ship in the waist, and rushing over the deck, banged against our sky-light, and bounced into our cabin. Three women were immediately apparent from their respective cribs, and poor H—— appeared in all her lengthy full-length, and came and took refuge with me. As I held her in my arms, and put my cloak round her, she shook from head to foot, poor child!—I was not the least frightened, but rather excited by this invasion of Dan Neptune's; but I wish to goodness I had been on deck.—Oh, how I wish I had seen that spoonful of salt water flung from the sea's boiling bowl! I heard afterwards, that it had nearly washed away poor Mr. ——, besides handsomely ducking and frightening our military man. Lay all day on my back, most wretched, the ship heaving like any earthquake; in fact, there is something irresistibly funny in the way in which people seem dispossessed of their power of volition by this motion, rushing hither and thither in all directions but the one they purpose going, and making as many angles, fetches, and sidelong deviations from the point they aim at, as if the devil had tied a string to their legs and jerked it every now and then in spite — by the by, not a bad illustration of our mental and moral struggles towards their legitimate aims. Another horrible night ! oh horror !

Wednesday, 22d.

A fair wind—a fine day—though very, very cold and damp. It seems, in our squall last night, we had also a small piece of mutiny. During the mate's watch, and while the storm was at the worst, the man who was steering left the helm, and refused to obey orders; whereupon Mr. Curtis took up a hatchet, and assured him he would knock his brains out,—which the captain said, had it been his watch, he should have done on the spot, and without further warning.—We are upon the Newfoundland banks, though not yet on soundings. Stitched my gown — worked at my nightcap — walked about : — Mr. —— read Quentin Durward to us while we worked. The extreme cold made us take refuge in our cabin, where I sat working and singing till dinnertime. Dined at table again; afterwards came back to our cabin — began writing journal, and was interrupted by hearing a bustle in the dinner-room. The gentlemen were all standing up, and presently I heard Walter Scott's name passed round:—it made me lay down my pen. Oh! how pleasant it sounded—that unanimous blessing of strangers upon a great and good man, thus far from him—from all but our own small community. The genuine and spontaneous tribute to moral worth and mental power! Poor, poor Sir Walter! And yet no prayer that can be breathed to bless, no grateful and soul-felt invocation can snatch him from the common doom of earth-born flesh, or buy away one hour's anguish and prostration of body and spirit, before the triumphant infirmities of our miserable nature. I thought of Dante's lines, that I read but a day ago; and yet — and yet — fame is something. His fame is good — is great — is glorious. To be enshrined in the hearts of all virtuous and wise men, as the friend of virtue and the teacher of wisdom; to have freely given pleasure, happiness, forgetfulness, to millions of his fellow-creatures; to have made excellence lovely, and enjoyment pure and salutary; to have taught none but lessons of honour and integrity; to have surrounded his memory, and filled the minds of all men with images fair, and bright, and wonderful, yet left around his name no halo, and in the hearts of others no slightest cloud to blot these enchanting creations; to have done nothing but good with God's good gifts—is not this fame worth something? 'T is worth man's love, and God's approval—'t is worth toiling for, living for, and dying for. He has earned it fairly—he is a great and good man—peace be with him in his hour of mortal sorrow, and eternal peace hereafter in the heaven to which he surely goes. — They then drank Washington Irving,—a gentle spirit, too. After working for some time more, came on deck, where we danced with infinite glee, disturbed only by the surpassing uproar of Colonel ——.

     *   *   *   *   *

     *   *   *   *   *

The only of our crew whom I cotton to fairly, are the ——, and that good-natured lad, Mr. ——; though the former rather distress me by their abundant admiration, and the latter by his inveterate Yorkshire, and never opening his mouth when he sings, which, as he has a very sweet voice, is a cruel piece of selfishness, keeping half his tones, and all his words for his own private satisfaction.

Thursday, 23d.

On soundings, and nearly off them again — a fine day ; — worked at my nightcap — another, by the by, having finished one — exemplary ! — Walked about, ate, drank, wrote journal — read some of it to the ——, who seemed much gratified by my doing so. I go on with Byron's life. He is too much of an egotist. I do not like him a bit the better for knowing his prose mind ; — far from thinking it redeems any of the errors of his poetical man, I think I never read any thing professing to be a person's undisguised feelings and opinions with so much heartlessness — so little goodness in it. His views of society are like his views of human nature ; or rather, by the by, reverse the sentence, to prove the fallacy in judgment ; and though his satire is keen and true, yet he is nothing but satirical — never, never serious and earnest, even with himself. Oh ! I have a horror of that sneering devil of Goëthe's ; and he seems to me to have possessed Byron utterly. A curious thought, or rather a fantastical shadow of a thought, occurred to me to-day in reading a chapter in the Corinthians about the resurrection. I mean to be buried

with H——'s ring on my finger; will it be there
when I rise again? — What a question for the
discussers of the needle's point controversy. My
father read to us, this afternoon, part of one of
Webster's speeches. It was very eloquent, but
yet it did not fulfil my idea of perfect oratory
— inasmuch as I thought it too pictorial: — there
was too much scenery and decoration about it, to
use the cant of my own trade; — there was too
much effect, theatrical effect in it, from which
Heaven defend me, for I do loathe it *in* its place,
and fifty times worse out of it. Perhaps Webster's speaking is a good sample, in its own line,
of the leaven wherewith these times are leavened.
I mean only in its defects — for its merits are
sterling, and therefore of all time.

But this oil and canvass style of thinking, writing, and speaking, is bad. I wish our age were
more sculptural in its genius — though I have not
the power in any thing to conform thereto, I have
the grace to perceive its higher excellence; yet
Milton was a sculptor, Shakspeare a painter. How
do we get through that? — My reason for object-
ing to Webster's style — though the tears were
in my eyes several times while my father read —
is precisely the same as my reason for not altogether liking my father's reading, — 't is slightly

theatrical — something too much of passion, something too much of effect—but perhaps I am mistaken; for I do so abhor the slightest approach to the lamps and orange peel, that I had almost rather hear a " brazen candlestick turned on a wheel," than all the music of due emphasis and inflection, if allied to a theatrical manner. — Dined at table again. They abound in toasts, and, among others, gave " The friends we have left, and those we are going to !" My heart sank. I am going to no friend ; and the " stranger," with which the Americans salute wayfarers through their land, is the only title I can claim amongst them. After dinner, walked about — danced—saw the sun sink in a bed of gorgeous stormy clouds; — worked and walked till bedtime. — I was considerably amused, and my English blood a little roused at a very good-natured and well-meant caution of Mr.——, to avoid making an enemy of Colonel ——. He is, they say, a party man, having influence which he may exert to our detriment.

Friday, 24*th*.

Rose late after a fair night's sleep—came up to the round-house. After breakfast, worked and walked for an immense time. Read a canto in Dante : just as I had finished it, " A sail ! a sail !" was cried from all quarters. Remembering my promise to dear H——, I got together my writing materials, and scrawled her a few incoherent lines full of my very heart. The vessel bore rapidly down upon us, but as there was no pro-spect of either her or our lying-to, Mr. —— tied my missive, together with one Mr. —— had just scribbled, to a lump of lead, and presently we all rushed on deck to see the ship pass us. She was an English packet, from Valparaiso, bound to London; her foremast had been carried away, but she was going gallantly before the wind. As she passed us, Mr. —— got up into the boat to have a better chance of throwing. I saw him fling powerfully, — the little packet whizzed through the air, but the distance was impossible, and the dark waters received it within twenty feet of the ship, which sailed rapidly on, and had soon left us far behind. I believe I screamed, as the black sea closed over my poor letter.   *   *   *   *

*   *   *   *   *

*   *   *   *   *

Came down to my cabin and cried like a wretch —came up again, and found them all at lunch.

Went and lay on the bowsprit, watching the fair ship courtesying through the bright sea with all her sail set, a gallant and graceful sight. Came in—wrote journal—translated a German fable. Worked at my cap, while my father went on with Webster's speech. I am still of the same mind about it, though some of the passages he read to-day were finer than any I had heard before. He gets over a shallow descent with admirable plausibility—and yet I think I would rather be descended from a half heathen Saxon giant, than from William Penn himself. We dined at table again; D—— could not : she was ill. After dinner, sat working for some time :— I had a horrid sick headache,—walked on deck. The wind and sea were both rising; we stood by the side of the ship, and watched the inky waters swelling themselves, and rolling sullenly towards us, till they broke in silver clouds against the ship, and sprang above her sides, covering us with spray. The sky had grown mirk as midnight, and the wind that came rushing over the sea, was hot from the south. We staid out till it grew dark. At ten, the crazy old ship, in one of her headlong bounces, flung my whole supper in my lap; the wind and water were riotous; the ship plunged and shuddered. After screwing my

courage to a game of speculation, I was obliged to
leave it, and my companions. Came down and
went to bed. — Oh horror ! loathsome life ! —

Saturday and Sunday.

Towards evening got up and came on deck : —
tremendous head wind, going off our course;
pray Heaven we don't make an impromptu
landing on Sable Island ! Sat on the ship's side,
watching the huge ocean gathering itself up into
pitchy mountains, and rolling its vast ridges, one
after another, against the good ship, who dipped,
and dipped, and dived down into the black chasm,
and then sprang up again, and rode over the
swelling surges like an empress. The sky was
a mass of stormy black, here and there edged
with a copper-looking cloud, and breaking in one
or two directions into pale silvery strata, that had
an unhealthy lightning look : a heavy black squall
lay ahead of us, like a dusky curtain, whence
we saw the rain, fringe-like, pouring down against
the horizon. The wind blew furiously. I got
cradled among the ropes, so as not to be pitched
off when the ship lurched, and enjoyed it all
amazingly. It was sad and solemn, and, but for
the excitement of the savage-looking waves, that

every now and then lifted their overwhelming sides against us, it would have made me melancholy : but it stirred my spirits to ride over these huge sea-horses, that came bounding and bellowing round us. Remained till I was chilled with the bitter wind, and wet through with spray ;—walked up and down the deck for some time, — had scarce set foot within the round house, when a sea took her in midships, and soused the loiterers. Sat up, or rather slept up, till ten o'clock, and then went down to bed. I took up Pelham to-day for a second — 't is amazingly clever, and like the thing it means to be, to boot. Heard something funny that I wish to remember — at a Methodist meeting, the singer who led the Psalm tune, finding that his concluding word, which was Jacob, had not syllables enough to fill up the music adequately ended thus — Ja-a-a-a — Ja-a-a-a — fol-de-riddle — cob !—

Monday, 26th.

Read Byron's life ;— defend me from my friends ! Rose tolerably late ; after breakfast, took a walk on deck — lay and slept under our sea-tent ; read on until lunch-time — dined on deck,

—after dinner walked about with H—— and the captain; we had seated ourselves on the ship's side, but he being called away, we rushed off to the forecastle to enjoy the starlight by ourselves. We sat for a little time, but were soon found out; Mr. —— and Mr. —— joined us, and we sat till near twelve o'clock, singing and rocking under the stars. Venus—"The star of love, all stars above," —threw a silver column down the sea, like the younger sister of the moon's reflection. By the by, I saw to-day, and with delight, an American sunset. The glorious god strode down heaven's hill, without a cloud to dim his downward path; —as his golden disk touched the panting sea, I turned my head away, and in less than a minute he had fallen beneath the horizon—leapt down into the warm waves, and left one glow of amber round half the sky; upon whose verge, where the violet curtain of twilight came spreading down to meet its golden fringe,

> " The maiden,
> With white fire laden,
> Whom mortals call the moon,"

stood, with her silver lamp in her hand, and her pale misty robes casting their wan lustre faintly around her. Oh me, how glorious it was! how sad, how very, very sad I was!   *

  * * * * *

  * * * * *

Dear, yet forbidden thoughts, that from my soul,
While shines the weary sun, with stern control
I drive away; why, when my spirits lie
Shrouded in the cold sleep of misery,
Do ye return, to mock me with false dreaming,
Where love, and all life's happiness is beaming?
Oh visions fair! that one by one have gone
Down, 'neath the dark horizon of my days;
Let not your pale reflection linger on
In the bleak sky, where live no more your rays.
Night! silent nurse, that with thy solemn eyes
Hang'st o'er the rocking cradle of the world,
Oh! be thou darker to my dreaming eyes;
Nor, in my slumbers, be the past unfurl'd.
Haunt me no more with whisperings from the dead,
The dead in heart, the chang'd, the withered:
Bring me no more sweet blossoms from my spring,
Which round my soul their early fragrance fling,
And, when the morning, with chill icy start,
Wakes me, hang blighted round my aching heart:
Oh night, and slumber, be ye visionless,
Dark as the grave, deep as forgetfulness!

  * * * * *

  * * * * *

Night, thou shalt nurse me, but be sure, good nurse,
While sitting by my bed, that thou art silent,

I will not let thee sing me to my slumbers
With the sweet lullabies of former times,
Nor tell me tales, as other gossips wont,
Of the strange fairy days, that are all gone.

Wednesday, 28*th.*

Skipped writing on Tuesday — so much the
better— a miserable day spent between heart-ache
and side-ache.   *   *   *
          *   *   *   *   *

Rose late, breakfasted with H——, afterwards
went and sat on the forecastle, where I worked
the whole morning, woman's work, stitching. It
was intensely hot till about two o'clock, when a
full east wind came on, which the sailors all
blessed, but which shook from its cold wings a
heavy, clammy, chilly dew, that presently pierced
all our clothes, and lay on the deck like rain.
At dinner we were very near having a scene:
the Bostonian and the Jacksonite falling out
again about the President; and a sharp, quick,
snapping conversation, which degenerated into a
snarl on one side, and a growl on the other, for
a short time rather damped the spirits of the
table.   Here, at least, General Jackson seems very
unpopular, and half the company echoed in ear-

nest what I said in jest to end the dispute, " Oh hang General Jackson !" After dinner, returned to the forecastle with H—— to see the sun set; her brother followed us thither.   *

  *   *   *   *   *

Finished my work, and then, tying on sundry veils and handkerchiefs, danced on deck for some time; — I then walked about with ——, by the light of the prettiest young moon imaginable.   *

  *   *   *   *   *

Afterwards sat working and stifling in the round-house till near ten, and then, being no longer able to endure the heat, came down, undressed, and sat luxuriously on the ground in my dressing-gown drinking lemonade. At twelve went to bed; the men kept up a horrible row on deck half the night; singing, dancing, whooping, and running over our heads.   *   *   *

  *   *   *   *   *

The captain brought me to-day a land-swallow, which having flown out so far, came hovering exhausted over the ship, and suffered itself to be caught. Poor little creature ! how very much more I do love all things than men and women ! I felt sad to death for its weary little wings and frightened heart, which beat against my hand, without its having strength to struggle. I made a cage in a basket for it, and gave it some seed, which it will not eat — little carnivorous wretch! I must catch some flies for it.

Thursday, 29th.

My poor little bird is dead. I am sorry! I could mourn almost as much over the death of a soulless animal, as I would rejoice at that of a brute with a soul. Life is to these winged things a pure enjoyment; and to see the rapid pinions folded, and the bright eye filmed, conveys sadness to the heart, for 'tis almost like looking on — what indeed is not — utter cessation of existence. Poor little creature! I wished it had not died — I would but have borne it tenderly and carefully to shore, and given it back to the air again!

*   *   *   *   *

I sat down stairs in my cabin all day; the very spirit of doggerel possessed me, and I poured forth rhymes as rapidly as possible, and they were as bad as possible. — Wrote journal; in looking over my papers, fell in with the Star of Seville — some of it is very good. I'll write an English tragedy next. Dined at table — our heroes have drunk wine, and are amicable. After dinner, went on deck, and took short walk; saw a the sun set, which he did like a god, as he is, leaving the sky like a geranium curtain, which overshadowed the sea with rosy light — beautiful! Came down and sat on the floor like a Turkish woman, stitching, singing, and talking, till midnight; supped — and to bed. My appetite seems like the Danaïdes' tub, of credible memory.

* * * * *

* * * * *

Friday, 30th.

On soundings. A fog and a calm. Sky yellow, sea grey, dripping, damp, dingy, dark, and very disagreeable. Sat working, reading, and talking in our own cabin all day. Read part of a book called Adventures of a Younger Son. The gentlemen amused themselves with fishing, and brought up sundry hake and dog-fish. I examined the heart of one of the fish, and was surprised at the long continuance of pulsation after the cessation of existence. In the evening, sang, talked, and played French blind man's buff; — sat working till near one o'clock, and reading Moore's Fudge Family, — which is good fun. It's too hard to be becalmed within thirty hours of our destination.

*　　　*　　　*　　　*　　　*

*　　　*　　　*　　　*　　　*

Why art thou weeping
Over the happy, happy dead,
Who are gone away,
From this life of clay,
From this fount of tears,
From this burthen of years,
From sin, from sorrow,
From sad " to-morrow,"
From struggling and creeping :
Why art thou weeping,
Oh fool, for the dead ?

Why art thou weeping,
Over the steadfast faithful dead,
Who can never change,
Nor grow cold and strange,
Nor turn away,
In a single day,
From the love they bore,
And the faith they swore,
Who are true for ever,
Will slight thee never,
But love thee still,
Through good and ill,
With the constancy
Of eternity :
Why art thou weeping,
Oh fool, for the dead ?

They are your only friends ;
For where this foul life ends,
Alone beginneth truth, and love, and faith ;
All which sweet blossoms are preserved by death.

Saturday, 31*st.*

Becalmed again till about two o'clock, when a
fair wind sprang up, and we set to rolling before
it like mad. How curious it is to see the ship,
like a drunken man, reel through the waters,
pursued by that shrill scold the wind. Worked
at my handkerchief, and read aloud to them
Mrs. Jameson's book.   *   *   *
    *   *   *   *   *

Set my foot half into a discussion about Portia,
but withdrew it in time. Lord bless us ! what
foul nonsense people do talk, and what much
fouler nonsense it is to answer them. Got
very sick, and lay on the ground till dinner-
time; went to table, but withdrew again while it
was yet in my power to do so gracefully. Lay on
the floor all the evening, singing for very sea-
sickness; suddenly it occurred to me, that it was
our last Saturday night on board; whereupon I
indited a song to the tune of " To Ladies' eyes
around, boys"—and having duly instructed Mr.
—— how to "speak the speech," we went to supper. *Last — last —* dear, dear, what is there in

that word! I don't know one of this ship's company, don't care for some of them — I have led a loathsome life in it for a month past, and yet the *last* Saturday night seemed half sad to me. Mr. —— sang my song and kept my secret: the song was encored, and my father innocently demanded the author; I gave him a tremendous pinch, and looked very silly. Merit, like murder, will out; so I fancy that when they drank the health of the author, the whole table was aware of the genius that sat among them. They afterwards sang a clever parody of " To all ye ladies now at land," by Mr. ——, the " canny Scot," who has kept himself so quiet all the way. Came to bed at about half-past twelve; while undressing, I heard the captain come down stairs and announce that we were clear of Nantucket shoal, and within one hundred and fifty miles of New York, which intelligence was received with three cheers. They continued to sing and shout till very late.

SATURDAY NIGHT SONG.

Come fill the can again, boys,
One parting glass, one parting glass ;
Ere we shall meet again, boys,
Long years may pass, long years may pass.

We'll drink the gallant bark, boys,
That's borne us through, that's borne us through,
Bright waves and billows dark, boys,
Our ship and crew, our ship and crew.

We'll drink those eyes that bright, boys,
With smiling ray, with smiling ray,
Have shone like stars to light, boys,
Our wat'ry way, our wat'ry way.
We'll drink our English home, boys,
Our father land, our father land,
And the shores to which we're come, boys,
A sister strand, a sister strand.

Sunday, September 2d.

Rose at half-past six: the sun was shining brilliantly; woke H—— and went on deck with her. The morning was glorious, the sun had risen two hours in the sky, the sea was cut by a strong breeze, and curled into ridges that came like emerald banks crowned with golden spray round our ship; she was going through the water at nine knots an hour. I sat and watched the line of light that lay like a fairy road to the east—towards my country, my dear, dear home. * * * *
* * * * *

Breakfasted at table for the first time since I've been on board the ship—I did hope, the last. After breakfast, put my things to rights, tidied our cabin for prayers, and began looking out the lessons; while doing so, the joyful sound, " Land, land!" was heard aloft. I rushed on deck, and between the blue waveless sea, and the bright unclouded sky, lay the wished-for line of darker element. 'T was Long Island: through a glass I descried the undulations of the coast, and even the trees that stood relieved against the sky. Hail, strange land! my heart greets you coldly and sadly! Oh, how I thought of Columbus, as with eyes strained and on tiptoe our water-weary passengers stood, after a summer's sail of thirty days, welcoming their mother earth! The day was heavenly, though intensely hot, the sky utterly cloudless, and by that same token, I do not love a cloudless sky. They tell me that this is their American weather almost till Christmas; that's nice, for those who like frying. Commend me to dear England's soft, rich, sad, harmonious skies and foliage — commend me to the misty curtain of silver vapour that hangs over her September woods at morning, and shrouds them at night;—in short, I am home-sick before touching land. After lunch, my father read prayers to us, and that excellent sermon of dear Mr. Thurstone's on taking the sacrament. After prayers, came on deck; there were two or three sails in sight — hailed a schooner which passed us — bad news of the cholera — pleasant this — walked about, collected goods and chattels, wrote journal, spent some time in seeing a couple of geese take a sea-swim with strings tied to their legs. After dinner, sat in my cabin some time — walked on deck; when the gentlemen joined us we danced the sun down, and the moon up. The sky was like the jewel-shop of angels; I never saw such brilliant stars nor so deep an azure to hang them in. The moon was grown powerful, and flooded the deck, where we sat playing at blind man's buff, magic music, and singing, and talking of shore till midnight, when we came to bed. I must not forget how happy an omen greeted us this morning. As we stood watching the "*dolce color di oriental zaffiro,*" one of the wild wood pigeons of America flew round our mizen-mast, and alighted on the top-sail yard; — this was the first living creature which welcomed us to the New World, and it pleased my superstitious fancy. I would have given any thing to have caught the bird, but after resting itself awhile, it took flight again and left us. We were talking to-day to one of our steerage passengers, a Huddersfield manufacturer, going out in quest of a living, with five children of his own to take care of, and two nephews. The father of the latter, said our Yorkshireman, having married a second time, and these poor children being as it were " *thristen* (thrust) out into the world loike—whoy oi jist took care of them." Verily, verily, he will have his reward—these tender mercies of the poor to one another are beautiful, and most touching.

Monday, September 3d.

I had desired the mate to call me by sunrise, and accordingly, in the midst of a very sound and satisfactory sleep, Mr. Curtis shook me roughly by the arm, informing me that the sun was just about to rise. The glorious god was quicker at his toilet than I at mine; for though I did but put on a dressing-gown and cloak, I found him come out of his eastern chamber, arrayed like a bridegroom, without a single beam missing. I called H——, and we remained on deck watching the clouds like visions of brightness and beauty, enchanted creations of some strange spell-land—at every moment assuming more fantastic shapes and gorgeous tints. Dark rocks seemed to rise, with dazzling summits of light, pale lakes of purest blue spread here and there between — the sun now shining through a white wreath of floating silver, now firing, with a splendour that the eye shrank from, the edges of some black cloudy mass. Oh, it was surpassing ! — We were becalmed, however, which rather damped all our spirits, and half made the captain swear. Towards mid-day we had to thank Heaven for an incident. A brig had been standing aft against the horizon for some hours past, and we presently descried a boat rowing from her towards us. The distance was some five miles, the sun broiling, we telescoped and stood on tiptoe, they rowed stoutly, and in due time boarded us. She was an English brig from Bristol, had been out eleven weeks, distressed by contrary winds, and was in want of provisions. The boat's crew was presently surrounded, grog was given the men, porter to the captain and his companion. Our dear captain supplied them with every thing they wanted, and our poor steerage passengers sent their mite to the distressed crew in the shape of a sack of potatoes; they remained half an hour on board, we clustering round them, questioning and answering might and main. As H—— said, they were new faces at least, and though two of the most ill-favoured physiognomies I ever set eyes on, there was something refreshing even in their ugly novelty. After this the whole day was one of continual excitement, nearing the various points of land, greeting vessels passing us, and watching those bound on the same course. At about four o'clock a schooner came alongside with a news collector; he was half devoured with queries; news of the cholera, reports of the tariff and bank questions were loudly demanded: poor people, how anxiously, they looked for replies to the first! Mr. ——, upon whose arm I leant, turned pale as death while asking how it had visited Boston. Poor fellow! poor people all! my heart ached with their anxiety. As the evening darkened, the horizon became studded with sails; at about eight o'clock we discovered the Highlands of Neversink, the entrance to New York harbour, and presently the twin lights of Sandy Hook glimmered against the sky. We were all in high spirits, a fresh breeze had sprung up, we were making rapidly to land; the lovely ship, with all sail set, courtesying along the smooth waters. The captain alone seemed anxious, and was eagerly looking out for the pilot. Some had gathered to the ship's side, to watch the progress of Colonel ——, who had left us and gone into the news-boat, which was dancing like a fairy by the side of our dark vessel. Cheering resounded on all sides, rockets were fired from the ship's stern, we were all dancing, when suddenly a cry was echoed round of " A pilot, a pilot!" and close under the ship's side a light graceful little schooner shot like an arrow through the dim twilight, followed by a universal huzza; she tacked, and lay to, but proved only a news-boat: while, however, all were gathered round the collector, the pilot-boat came alongside, and the pilot on board; the captain gave up the cares and glories of command, and we danced an interminable country dance. All was excitement and joyous confusion; poor Mr. —— alone seemed smitten with sudden anxiety; the cholera reports had filled him with alarm, lest his agent should have died, and his affairs on his arrival be in confusion and ruin — poor fellow ! I was very sorry for him. We went down to supper at ten, and were very merry, in spite of the ship's bumping twice or thrice upon the sands. Came up and dawdled upon deck — saw them cast anchor ; away went the chain, down dropped the heavy stay, the fair ship swung round, and there lay new York before us, with its clustered lights shining like a distant constellation against the dark outline of land. Remained on deck till very late — were

going to bed, when the gentlemen entreated us to
join their party once more; we did so, sang all the
old songs, laughed at all the old jokes, drank our
own and each other's health, wealth, and prosperity, and came to bed at two o'clock. Our cradle
rocks no longer, but lies still on the still waters;
we have reached our destination; thank God! I
did so with all my soul.

> *Tuesday, September 4th,*
> *New York, America.*

It is true, by my faith! it is true; there it is
written, here I sit, I am myself and no other,
this is New York and nowhere else—Oh! "singular, strange!" Our passengers were all stirring
and about at peep of day, and I got up myself at
half past six. Trunks lay scattered in every
direction around, and all were busily preparing to
leave the good ship Pacific. Mercy on us!
it made me sad to leave her and my shipmates.
I feel like a wretch swept down a river to the
open sea, and catch at the last boughs that hang
over the banks to stay me from that wide loneli-
ness. The morning was real Manchester. I believe some of the passengers had brought the fog
and rain in their English clothes, which they

were all putting on, together with best hats, dandy cravats, &c. — to make a *sensation.* A fog hung over the shores of Staten Island and Long Island, in spite of which, and a dreary, heavy, thick rain, I thought the hilly outline of the former very beautiful; the trees and grass were rather sunburnt, but in a fair spring day I should think it must be lovely. We breakfasted, and packed ourselves into our shawls and bonnets, and at half-past nine the steam-boat came alongside to take us to shore: it was different from any English steam-boat I ever saw, having three decks, and being consequently a vessel of very considerable size. We got on board her all in the rain and misery, and as we drifted on, our passengers collected to the side of the boat and gave "The dear old Lady" three cheers. Poor ship! there she lay — all sails reefed, rocking in melancholy inaction, deserted by her merry inmates, lonely and idle — poor Pacific! I should like to return in that ship; I would willingly skip a passage in order to do so. All were looking at the shores; some wondering and admiring, others recognising through the rain and mist, as best they might; I could not endure to lift my eyes to the strange land, and even had I done so, was crying too bitterly to see any thing. Mr. ——

and Mr. —— went to secure apartments for us at the American Hotel; and after bidding good-by to the sea, we packed ourselves into a hackney coach, and progressed.   The houses are almost all painted glaring white or red; the other favourite colours appear to be pale straw colour and grey.   They have all green venetian shutters, which give an idea of coolness, and almost every house has a tree or trees in its vicinity, which looks pretty and garden-like.   We reached our inn, — the gentlemen were waiting for us, and led us to our drawing-room.   I had been choking for the last three hours, and could endure no more, but sobbed like a wretch aloud.   *   *

          *   *   *   *   *

There was a piano in the room, to which I flew with the appetite of one who has lived on the music of the speaking-trumpet for a month; that, and some iced lemonade and cake, presently restored my spirits.   I went on playing and singing till I was exhausted, and then sat down and wrote journal.   Mr. —— went out and got me Sir Humphry Davy's Salmonia, which I had been desiring, and he had been speaking of on board ship.

At five o'clock we all met once more together to dinner.   Our drawing-room being large and pleasant, the table was laid in it. 'T is curious how an acquaintanceship of thirty days has contrived to bind together in one common feeling of kindness and good-fellowship persons who never met before, who may never meet again. To-morrow we all separate to betake ourselves each to our several path; and as if loath to part company, they all agreed to meet once more on the eve of doing so, probably for ever. How strongly this clinging principle is inherent in our nature! These men have no fine sympathies of artificial creation, and this exhibition of *adhesiveness* is in them a real and heart-sprung feeling. It touched me — indeed it may well do so; for friends of thirty days are better than utter strangers, and when these my shipmates shall be scattered abroad, there will be no human being left near us whose face we know, or whose voice is familiar to us. Our dinner was a favourable specimen of eating as practised in this new world; every thing good, only in too great a profusion, the wine drinkable, and the fruit beautiful to look at: in point of flavour it was infinitely inferior to English hothouse fruit, or even fine espalier fruit raised in a good aspect. Every thing was wrapped in ice, which is a most luxurious necessary in this hot climate; but the

things were put on the table in a slovenly, out-
landish fashion; fish, soup, and meat, at once,
and puddings, and tarts, and cheese, at another
once; no finger glasses, and a patched table-
cloth, — in short, a want of that style and neatness which is found in every hotel in England.
The waiters, too, reminded us of the half-savage
Highland lads that used to torment us under that
denomination in Glasgow — only that they were
wild Irish instead of wild Scotch. The day had
cleared, and become intensely hot, towards evening softening and cooling under the serene influences of the loveliest moon imaginable. The
streets were brilliantly lighted, the shops through
the trees, and the people parading between them,
reminded me very much of the Boulevards. We
left the gentlemen, and went down stairs, where
I played and sang for three hours. On opening
the door, I found a junta of men sitting on the
hall floor, round it, and smoking. Came up for
coffee; most of the gentlemen were rather elated,
— we sang, and danced, and talked, and seemed
exceeding loath to say good-by. I sat listening
to the dear Doctor's theory of the nature of
the soul, which savoured infinitely more of the
spirituality of the bottle than of immaterial exist-
ences. I heard him descant very tipsily upon

the vital principle, until my fatigue getting fairly the better of my affection for him, I bade our remaining guests good night, and came to bed.

Wednesday, 5th.

I have been in a sulky fit half the day, because people will keep walking in and out of our room, without leave or licence, which is coming a great deal too soon to Hope's idea of Heaven. I am delighted to see my friends, but I like to tell them so, and not that they should take it for granted. When I made my appearance in my dressing gown, (my clothes not being come, and the day too hot for a silk pelisse,) great was my amazement to find our whole ship's company assembled at the table. After breakfast they dispersed, and I sat writing journal, and playing, and singing. Colonel —— and Mr. —— called. Our Boston friends leave us to-day for their homes. I am sorry to lose them, though I think H—— will be the better for rest. Mrs. —— called to see D—— to-day. I remember her name, as one of the first things I do remember. A visit from a Mr. ——, one of the directors of the Custom-House, and W—— P——, brother to the proprietor of the Park theatre, who is a lawyer of considerable reputation here. The face of the first was good, the other's clever. I said nothing, as usual, and let them depart in peace. We dined at half-past two, with the H——s and Mr. ——. At half-past three we walked down to the quay to convoy them to their steamboat, which looked indeed like a "castle on the main." We saw them on board, went down and looked at the state cabin, which was a magnificent room, and would have done charmingly for a galoppade. We bade our new friends, whom I like better than some old ones, good-by, and walked briskly on to the battery, to see them as they passed it. The sun was intensely hot; and as I struggled forward, hooked up to this young Sheffield giant, I thought we were the living illustration of Hood's "Long and Short" of it. We gained the battery, and saw the steam-boat round; our travellers kept the deck with "hat and glove and handkerchief," as long as we could see them. This battery is a beautiful marine parade, commanding the harbour and entrance of the bay, with Governor's Island, and its dusky red fort, and the woody shores of New Jersey and Long Island. A sort of public promenade, formed of grass plots, planted with a variety of trees, affords a very agreeable position from whence to enjoy the lovely view. My companion informed me that this was a fashionable resort some time ago; but owing to its being frequented by the lowest and dirtiest of the rabble, who in this land of liberty roll themselves on the grass, and otherwise annoy the more respectable portion of the promenaders, it has been much deserted lately, and is now only traversed by the higher classes as a thoroughfare. The trees and grass were vividly and luxuriantly green; but the latter grew rank and long, unshorn and untidy. "Oh," thought I, "for a pair of English shears, to make these green carpets as smooth and soft and thick as the close piled Genoa velvet." It looked neglected and slovenly. Came home up Broadway, which is a long street of tolerable width, full of shops, in short the American Oxford Road, where all people go to exhibit themselves and examine others. The women that I have seen hitherto have all been very gaily dressed, with a pretension to French style, and a more than English exaggeration of it. They all appear to me to walk with a French shuffle, which, as their pavements are flat, I can only account for by their wearing shoes made in the French fashion, which are enough in themselves to make a waddler of the best walker that ever set foot to earth. Two or three were pretty girls; but the town being quite empty, these are probably bad specimens of the graces and charms that adorn Broadway in its season of shining. Came home and had tea; after which my father, I, and Mr. —— crossed the Park (a small bit of grass enclosed in white palings, in plain English, a green) to the theatre. Wallack was to act in the Rent Day. Mercy, how strange I felt as I once more set foot in a theatre; the sound of the applause set my teeth on edge. The house is pretty though rather gloomy, well formed, about the size of the Haymarket, with plenty of gold carving, and red silk about it, looking rich and warm. The audience was considerable, but all men; scarce, I should think, twenty women in the dress circle, where, by the by, as well as in the private boxes, I saw men sitting with their hats on. The Rent Day is a thorough melodrama, only the German monster has put on a red waistcoat and top boots. Nathless this is a good thing of a bad sort: the incidents, though not all probable, or even as skilfully tacked together as they might be, are striking and dramatically effective, and the whole piece turns on those home feelings, those bitterest realities of every-day life, that wring one's heart, beyond the pain that one allows works of fiction to excite. As for the imitation of Wilkie's pictures, the first was very pretty, but the second I did not see, my face being buried in my handkerchief, besides having a quarter less seven fathom of tears over it, at the time. I cried most bitterly during the whole piece; for as in his very first scene Wallack asks his wife if she will go with him to America, and she replies, " What ! leave the farm ?" I set off from thence and ceased no more. The manager's wife and another woman were in the box, which was his, and I thought we should have carried away the front of it with our tears. Wallack played admirably : I had never seen him before, and was greatly delighted with his acting. I thought him handsome of a rustic kind, the very thing for the part he played, a fine English yeoman : he reminded me of ——. At the end of the play, came home with a tremendous headache : sat gossiping and drinking lemonade. Presently a tap at the door came, and through the door came Mr. ——. I shook hands with him, and began expatiating on the impertinence of people's not enquiring down stairs whether we were at home or not before they came up — I don't believe he took my idea. Mr. —— came in to bid us good-by : he starts to-morrow for Baltimore. He is a nice, good-tempered young Irishman, with more tongue than brains, but still clever enough : I am sorry he is going. Came to bed-room at eleven, remained up till one, unpacking goods and chattels. Mercy on me, what a cargo it is! They have treated us like ambassadors, and not one of our one and twenty huge boxes have been touched.

Thursday, 6th.

Rose at eight. After breakfast, began writing to my brother; while doing so they brought up Captain ——'s and Mr. ——'s cards. I was delighted to see our dear Captain again, who, in spite of his glorious slip-slop, is a glorious fellow. They sat some time. Colonel —— called, — he walks my father off his legs. When they were all gone, finished letter and wrote journal. Unpacked and sorted things. Opened with a trembling heart my bonnet box, and found my precious *Dévy* squeezed to a crush — I pulled it out, rebowed, and reblonded, and reflowered it, and now it looks good enough " pour les *th*auvages mam*the*lle Fannie." Worked at my muslin gown; in short, did a deal. A cheating German woman came here this morning with some bewitching canezous and pelerines: I chose two that I wanted, and one very pretty one that I didn't; but as she asked a heathen price for 'em, I took only the former; — dear good little me!* We dined at five. After dinner, sang and played to my father, "all by the light of the moon." The evening was, as the day had been, lovely; and as I stood by his side near the open window, and saw him inhaling the pure fresh air, which he said invigorated and revived him, and heard him exclaim upon the beauty of our surroundings, half of my regret for this exile melted away.   *

*   *   *   *   *

*   *   *   *   *

He said to me, "Is there not reason to be grateful to God, when we look at these fair things?" — and indeed, indeed, there is: yet these things are not to me what they were. He told me that he had begun a song on board ship for the last Saturday night, but that not feeling well he had given it up, but the very same ideas I had made use of had occurred to him.   *   *   *

*   *   *   *   *

* I do not know how it is to be accounted for, but in spite of much lighter duties, every article of dress, particularly silks, embroideries, and all French manufactures, are more expensive here than in England. The extravagance of the American women in this part of their expenditure is, considering the average fortunes of this country, quite extraordinary. They never walk in the streets but in the most showy and extreme toilette, and I have known twenty, forty, and sixty dollars paid for a bonnet to wear in a morning saunter up Broadway.

This is not surprising; the ideas were so obvious that there was no escaping them. My
father is ten years younger since he came here,
already.   *   *   *   *   *
        *   *   *   *   *

Colonel —— came in after tea, and took my
father off to the Bowery theatre. I remained
with D—— singing, and stitching, and gossiping till twelve o'clock. My father has been introduced to half the town, and tells me that far
from the democratic *Mister*, which he expected
to be every man's title here, he had made the
acquaintance of a score of municipal dignitaries,
and some sixty colonels and major-generals — of
militia. Their omnibuses are vehicles of rank,
and the *Ladies* Washington, Clinton, and Van
Rensalear *, rattle their crazy bones along the
pavement for all the world like any other old
women of quality.

These democrats are as title-sick as a banker's
wife in England. My father told me to-day, that
Mr. ——, talking about the state of the country,
spoke of the lower orders finding their level:
now this enchants me, because a republic is a
natural anomaly; there is nothing republican in
the construction of the material universe; there

* These are the titles of three omnibuses which run up
and down Broadway all the day long.

be highlands and lowlands, lordly mountains as barren as any aristocracy, and lowly valleys as productive as any labouring classes. The feeling of rank, of inequality, is inherent in us, a part of the veneration of our natures; and like most of our properties seldom finds its right channels — in place of which it has created artificial ones suited to the frame of society into which the civilised world has formed itself. I believe in my heart that a republic is the noblest, highest, and purest form of government; but I believe that according to the present disposition of human creatures, 't is a mere beau ideal, totally incapable of realisation. What the world may be fit for six hundred years hence, I cannot exactly perceive ; but in the mean time, 't is my conviction that America will be a monarchy before I am a skeleton.

One of the curses of living at an inn in this unceremonious land: — Dr. ―― walked in this evening accompanied by a gentleman, whom he forthwith introduced to us. I behaved very *ill*, as I always do on these occasions; but 't is an impertinence, and I shall take good care to certify such to be my opinion of these free and easy proceedings. The man had a silly manner, but he may be a genius for all that. He abused General Jackson, and said the cholera was owing to his presidency; for that Clay had predicted, that when he came into

power, battle, pestilence, and famine, would come
upon the land: which prophecy finds its accomplishment thus: they have had a war with the Indians, the cholera has raged, and the people, flying from the infected cities to the country, have
eaten half the farmers out of house and home.
This hotel reminds me most extremely of our
"iligant" and untidy apartments in dear, nasty
Dublin, at the Shelbourne. The paper in our
bed-room is half peeling from the walls, our beds
are without curtains, then to be sure there are
pier looking-glasses, and one or two pieces of
showy French furniture in it. 'T is customary,
too, here, I find, for men to sleep three or four in
a room; conceive an Englishman shown into a
dormitory for half-a-dozen; I can't think how
they endure it; but, however, I have a fever at
all those things. My father asked me, this evening, to write a sonnet about the wild pigeons
welcoming us to America; I had thought of it
with scribbling intent before, but he wants me
to get it up here, and that sickened me.

Friday, 7th.

Rose at eight: after breakfast tidied my dressing-box, mended and tucked my white muslin
gown — wrote journal: while doing so, Colonel

—— came to take leave of us for a few days; he is going to join his wife in the country. Mr. —— called and remained some time; while he was here, the waiter brought me word that a Mr. —— wanted to see me. I sent word down that my father was out, knowing no such person, and supposing the waiter had mistaken whom he asked for; but the gentleman persisted in seeing me, and presently in walked a good-looking elderly man, who introduced himself as Mr. ——, to whom my father had letters of introduction. He sat himself down, and pottered a little, and then went away. When he was gone, Mr. —— informed me that this was one of *the* men of New York, in point of wealth, influence, and consideration. He had been a great auctioneer, but had retired from business, having, among his other honours, filled the office of Mayor of New York. My father and Mr. —— went to put our letters in the post: I practised and needle-worked till dinner-time; after dinner, as I stood at the window looking at the lovely sky, and the brilliant earth, a curious effect of light struck me. Within a hundred yards of each other, the Town Hall lay, with its white walls glowing in the sunset, while the tall grey church-steeple was turning pale in the clear moonlight. That Town Hall is a white-washed anomaly, and yet its effect is not altogether bad. I took a bath at the house behind it, which is very conveniently arranged for that purpose, with a French sort of gallery, all papered with the story of Psyche in lead-coloured paper, that reminded me of the doughy immortals I used to admire so much, at the inns at Abbeville and Montreuil. The house was kept by a foreigner — I knew it. My father proposed to us a walk, and we accordingly sallied forth. We walked to the end of Broadway, a distance of two miles, I should think, and then back again. The evening was most lovely. The moon was lighting the whole upper sky, but every now and then, as we crossed the streets that led to the river, we caught glimpses of the water, and woody banks, and the sky that hung over them; which all were of that deep orange tint, that I never saw, but in Claude's pictures. After walking nearly a mile up Broadway, we came to Canal Street: it is broader and finer than any I have yet seen in New York; and at one end of it, a Christian church, copied from some Pagan temple or other, looked exceedingly well, in the full flood of silver light that streamed from heaven. There were many temptations to look around, but the flags were so horribly broken and out of order,

that to do so was to run the risk of breaking one's
neck : — this is very bad.* The street was very
much thronged, and I thought the crowd a more
civil and orderly one, than an English crowd.
The men did not jostle or push one another, or
tread upon one's feet, or kick down one's shoe
heels, or crush one's bonnet into one's face, or
turn it round upon one's head, all which I have
seen done in London streets. There is this to be
said : this crowd was abroad merely for pleasure,
sauntering along, which is a thing never seen in
London; the proportion of idle loungers who frequent the streets there being very inconsiderable,
when compared with the number of people going
on business through the town. I observed that
the young men to-night invariably made room for
women to pass, and many of them, as they drew
near us, took the segar from their mouth, which I
thought especially courteous.† They were all

* The New Yorkers have begun to see the evil of their
ways, as far as regards their carriage-road in Broadway ; —
which is now partly Macadamised. It is devoutly to be
hoped, that the worthy authorities will soon have as much
compassion on the feet of their fellow-citizens, as they have
begun to have for their brutes.

† The roughness and want of refinement, which is legiti-
mately complained of in this country is often however miti-
gated by instances of civility, which would not be found
commonly elsewhere. As I have noticed above, the demean-

smoking, to a man, except those who were spitting, which helped to remind me of Paris, to which the whole place bore a slight resemblance. The shops appear to me to make no show whatever, and will not bear a comparison with the brilliant display of the Parisian streets, or the rich magnificence of our own, in that respect. The women dress very much, and very much like French women gone mad; they all of them seem to me to walk horribly ill, as if they wore tight shoes. Came in rather tired, took tea, sang an immensity, wrote journal, looked at the peerless moon, and now will go to bed.

Saturday, 8th.

Stitching the whole blessed day; and as I have now no maid to look after them, my clothes run some chance of being decently taken care of, and kept in order. Mr. ——— and his daughter called;

---

our of men towards women in the streets is infinitely more courteous here than with us; women can walk, too, with perfect safety, by themselves, either in New York, Philadelphia, or Boston: on board the steam-boats no person sits down to table until the ladies are accommodated with seats; and I have myself in church benefited by the civility of men who have left their pew, and stood, during the whole service, in order to afford me room.

I like him; he appears very intelligent; and the expression of his countenance is clever and agreeable. His daughter was dressed up in French clothes, and looked very stiff; but, however, a first visit is an awkward thing, and nothing that isn't thorough-bred ever does it quite well. When they were gone, Mr. —— called. By the by, of Mr. ——, while he was speaking, he came to the word *calculate*, and stopping half way, substituted another for it, which made me laugh internally. Mercy on me! how sore all these people are about Mrs. Trollope's book, and how glad I am I did not read it. She must have spoken the truth though, for lies do not rankle so.

    " Qui ne nous touche point, ne nous fait pas rougir."

Worked till dinner-time. —— dined with us: what a handsome man he is; but oh, what a within and without actor. I wonder whether I carry such a brand in every limb and look of me; if I thought so, I'd strangle myself. An actor shall be self-convicted in five hundred. There is a ceaseless striving at effect, a straining after points in talking, and a lamp and orange-peel twist in every action. How odious it is to me! Absolute and unmitigated vulgarity I can put up with, and welcome; but good Heaven defend me from the

genteel version of vulgarity, to see which in perfection, a country actor, particularly if he is also
manager, and sees occasionally people who be-
speak plays, is your best occasion. My dear
father, who was a little elated, made me sing to
him, which I greatly gulped at. When he was
gone, went on playing and singing. Wrote journal, and now to bed. I'm dead of the sideache.*

Sunday, 9th.

Rose at eight. While I was dressing, D——
went out of the room, and presently I heard
sundry exclamations : " Good God, is it you !
How are you ? How have you been ?" I opened
the door, and saw my uncle.   *   *

After breakfast, went to church with my father :
on our way thitherward, met the Doctor, and the
Doctor's friend, and Mr. ——, to whom I have
taken an especial fancy. The church we went to

---

* Saw a woman riding to-day ; but she has gotten a black
velvet beret upon her head. — Only think of a beret on horseback ! The horses here are none of them properly broken :
their usual pace being a wrong-legged half-canter, or a species
of shambling trot, denominated, with infinite justice, a *rack*.
They are all broken with snaffles instead of curbs, carry their
noses out, and pull horribly ; I have not yet seen a decen.
rider, either man or woman.

is situated half way between the Battery and our hotel. It is like a chapel in the exterior, being quite plain, and standing close in among the houses; the interior was large and perfectly simple. The town is filling, and the church was well attended. 'Tis long since I have heard the church service so well read; with so few vices of pronunciation, or vulgarisms of emphasis. Our own clergy are shamefully negligent in this point; and if Chesterfield's maxim be a good one in all cases, which it is, surely in the matter of the service of God's house 't is doubly so; they lose an immense advantage, too, by their slovenly and careless way of delivering the prayers, which are in themselves so beautiful, so eloquent, so full of the very spirit of devotion; that whereas, now, a congregation seems but to follow their leader, in gabbling them over as they do; were they so-lemnly, devoutly, and impressively read, many would feel and understand, what they now repeat mechanically, without attaching one idea to the words they utter. There was no clerk to assist in the service, and the congregation were as neg-lectful of the directions in the prayer-book, and as indolent and remiss in uttering the responses, as they are in our own churches; indeed, the absence of the clerk made the inaudibility of the congre-

gation's portion of the service more palpable than
it is with us.   The organ and chanting were very
good; infinitely superior to the performances of
those blessed little parish cherubim, who mono-
polise the praises of God in our churches, so
much to the suffering of all good Christians not
favoured with deafness.   The service is a little
altered — all prayers for our King, Queen, House
of Lords, Parliament, &c., of course omitted: in
lieu of which, they pray for the President and all
existing authorities.   Sundry repetitions of the
Lord's Prayer, and other passages, were left out;
they correct our English, too, substituting the
more modern phraseology of *those*, for the dear
old-fashioned *them*, which our prayer-book uses:
as, " spare thou *those*, O God," instead of " spare
thou *them*, O God, which confess their faults."
Wherever the word wealth occurs, too, these
zealous purists, connecting that word with no idea
but dollars and cents, have replaced it by a term
more acceptable to their comprehension, — prosperity, — therefore they say, " In all time of our
prosperity, (*i. c.* wealth,) in all time of our tribu-
lation," &c.   I wonder how these gentlemen
interpret the word commonwealth, or whether,
in the course of their reading, they ever met with
the word deprived of the final th; and if so, what

they imagined it meant.* Our prayers were desired for some one putting out to sea; and a very touching supplication to that effect was read, in which I joined with all my heart. The sermon would have been good, if it had been squeezed into half the compass it occupied; it was upon the subject of the late terrible visitations with which God has tried the world, and was sensibly and well delivered, only it had " damnable iteration." The day was like an oven; after church, came home. Mr. —— called, also Mr. ——, the Boston manager, who is longer than any human being I ever saw. Presently after, a visit from " his honour the Recorder," a twaddling old lawyer by the name of ——, and a silent young gentleman, his son. They were very droll. The lawyer talked the most; at every half sentence, however, quoting, complimenting, or appealing to " his honour the Recorder," a little, good-tempered, turnippy-looking man, who called me a female; and who, the other assured me, was the

* The spirit of independence, which is the common atmospheric air of America, penetrates into the churches, as well as elsewhere. In Boston, I have heard the Apostles' creed mutilated and altered; once by the omission of the passage " descended into hell," and another time, by the substitution of the words " descended into the place of departed spirits."

Chesterfieldian of New York (I don't know precisely what that means): what fun! Again I
had an opportunity of perceiving how thorough a
chimera the equality is, that we talk of as American. " There's no such thing," with a vengeance!
Here they were, talking of their aristocracy and
democracy; and I'm sure, if nothing else bore
testimony to the inherent love of *higher things*
which I believe exists in every human creature,
the way in which the lawyer dwelt upon the Duke
of Montrose, to whom, in Scotch kindred, he is
allied at the distance of some miles, and Lady
Loughborough, whom Heaven knows how he got
hold of, would have satisfied me, that a my Lord,
or my Lady, are just as precious in the eyes of
these levellers, as in those of Lord and Lady-
loving John Bull himself. They staid pottering a
long time. One thing his " honour the Recorder"
told me, which I wish to remember: that the
only way of preserving universal suffrage from
becoming the worst of abuses, was of course to edu-
cate the people*, for which purpose a provision is

---

* Unfortunately, this precaution does not fulfil its purpose; universal suffrage is a political fallacy: and will be one
of the stumbling-blocks in the path of this country's greatness. I do not mean that it will lessen her wealth, or injure
her commercial and financial resources; but it will be an in-

made by government; thus: a grant of land is given, the revenue of which being estimated, the population of the State are taxed to precisely the same amount; thus furnishing, between the government and the people, an equal sum for the education of all classes.* I do nothing but look out of window all the blessed day long: I did not think in my old age to acquire so Jezebel a trick; but the park (as they entitle the green opposite our windows) is so very pretty, and the streets so gay, with their throngs of smartly dressed women, and so amusing with their abundant proportion of black

---

superable bar to the progress of mental and intellectual cultivation — 't is a plain case of action and re-action. If the mass, *i. e.* the inferior portion, (for when was the mass not inferior?) elect their own governors, they will of course elect an inferior class of governors, and the government of such men will be an inferior government; that it may be just, honest, and rational, I do not dispute; but that it ever will be enlarged, liberal, and highly enlightened, I do not, and cannot, believe.

* I do not know, whether his honour the Recorder's information applied only to the state of New York, or included all the others; 't is not one of the least strange features, which this strange political process, the American government, presents, that each state is governed by its own laws; thus forming a most involved and complicated whole, where each part has its own individual machinery; or, to use a more celestial phraseology, its own particular system.

and white caricatures, that I find my window the most entertaining station in the world. Read Salmonia : the natural-history part of it is curious and interesting; but the local descriptions are beyond measure tantalising; and the " bites," five thousand times more so. Our ship-mate, Mr. ——, called : I was glad to see him. Poor man ! how we did *reel* him off his legs to be sure, — what fun it was ! My father dined out : D—— and I dined *tête-à-tête.* Poor D—— has not been well to-day : she is dreadfully bitten by the musquitoes, which, I thank their discrimination, have a thorough contempt for me, and have not come near me : the only things that bother me are little black ants, which I find in my wash-hand basin, and running about in all directions. I think the quantity of fruit brings them into the houses. After dinner, sat looking at the blacks parading up and down; most of them in the height of the fashion, with every colour in the rainbow about them. Several of the black women I saw pass had very fine figures; (the women here appear to me to be remarkably small, my own being, I should think, the average height;) but the contrast of a bright blue, or pink crape bonnet, with the black face, white teeth, and glaring blue whites of the eyes, is beyond description grotesque. The carriages here are all, to my taste, very ugly; hung very high from the ground, and of all manner of ungainly, old-fashioned shapes. Now this is where, I think, the Americans are to be quarrelled with: they are beginning at a time when all other nations are arrived at the highest point of perfection, in all matters conducive to the comfort and elegance of life: they go into these countries; into France, into our own dear little snuggery, from whence they might bring models of whatever was most excellent, and give them to their own manufacturers, to imitate or improve upon. When I see these awkward, un-comfortable vehicles swinging through the streets, and think of the beauty, the comfort, the strength, and lightness of our English-built carriages and cabs, I am much surprised at the want of emu-lation and enterprise, which can be satisfied with inferiority, when equality, if not superiority, would be so easy.* At seven o'clock, D—— and I

---

* Whoever pretends to write any account of " Men and Manners" in America must expect to find his own work give him the lie in less than six months; for both men and manners are in so rapid a state of progress that no record of their ways of being and doing would be found correct at the expiration of that term, however much so at the period of its writing. Broadway is not only partly Macadamised since first we arrived here, but there are actually to be seen in it

walked out together. The evening was very
beautiful, and we walked as far as Canal Street and
back. During our promenade, two fire engines
passed us, attended by the usual retinue of shouting children; this is about the sixth fire since
yesterday evening. They are so frequent here,
that the cry " Fire, fire ! " seems to excite neither
alarm nor curiosity, and except the above men-
tioned pains-taking juveniles, none of the inhabitants seem in the least disturbed by it.* We
prosecuted our walk down to the Battery, but
just as we reached it, we had to return, as 't was
tea-time. I was sorry: the whole scene was
most lovely. The moon shone full upon the trees
and intersecting walks of the promenade, and
threw a bright belt of silver along the water's
edge. The fresh night wind came over the broad
estuary, rippling it, and stirring the boughs with
its delicious breath. A building, which was once

now, two or three carriages of decent build, with hammer-
cloths, foot-boards, and even once or twice lately I have
seen footmen standing on those foot-boards ! ! !

* Perhaps one reason for the perfect coolness with which
a fire is endured in New York is the dexterity and courage
of the firemen: they are, for the most part, respectable
tradesmen's sons, who enlist in this service, rather than the
militia; and the vigilance and activity with which their duty
is discharged deserves the highest praise.

a fort, from whence the Americans fired upon our ships, is now turned into a sort of *café*, and was brilliantly lighted with coloured lamps, shining among the trees, and reflected in the water. The whole effect was pretty, and very Parisian. We came home, and had tea, after which Mr. —— came in. He told us, that we must not walk alone at night, for that we might get spoken to, and that a friend of his, seeing us go out without a man, had followed us the whole way, in order to see that nothing happened to us: this was very civil. Played and sang, and strove to make that stupid lad sing, but he was shy, and would not open his mouth, even the accustomed hair's breadth. At about eleven he went away; and we came to bed at twelve.

Monday, 10*th*.

Rose at eight. After breakfast wrote journal, and practised for an hour. —— called. I remember taking a great fancy to him about eight years ago, when I was a little girl in Paris; but, mercy, how he is aged! I wonder whether I am beginning to look old yet, for it seems to me that all the world's in wrinkles. My father went out

with him. Read a canto in Dante; also read
through a volume of Bryant's poetry, which Mr.
—— had lent us, to introduce us to the American
Parnassus.   I liked a great deal of it very well;
and I liked the pervading spirit of it much more,
which appears to me hopeful and bright, and what
the spirit of a poet should be; for in spite of all
De Stael's sayings, and Byron's doings, I hold that
melancholy is *not* essentially the nature of a poet.
Though instances may be adduced of great poets
whose Helicon has been but a bitter well of tears,
yet, in itself, the spirit of poetry appears to me to
be too strong, too bright, too full of the elements
of beauty and of excellence, too full of God's own
nature, to be dark or desponding; and though
from the very fineness of his mental constitution
a poet shall suffer more intensely from the baseness
and the bitterness which are the leaven of life,
yet he, of all men, the most possesses the power
to discover truth, and beauty, and goodness, where
they do exist; and where they exist not, to create
them.   If the clouds of existence are darker, its
sunshine is also brighter to him; and while others,
less gifted, lose themselves in the labyrinth of life,
his spirit should throw light upon the darkness,
and he should walk in peace and faith over the
stormy waters, and through the uncertain night;

standing as 't were above the earth, he views with clearer eyes its mysteries; he finds in apparent discord glorious harmony, and to him the sum of all is good; for, in God's works, good still abounds to the subjection of evil. 'T is this trustful spirit that seems to inspire Bryant, and to me, therefore, his poetry appears essentially good. There is not much originality in it. I scarce think there can be in poems so entirely descriptive: his descriptions are very beautiful, but there is some sameness in them, and he does not escape self-repetition; but I am a bad critic, for which I thank God! I know the tears rolled down my cheeks more than once as I read; I know that agreeable sensations and good thoughts were suggested by what I read; I thought some of it beautiful, and all of it wholesome (in contradistinction to the literature of this age), and I was well pleased with it altogether. Afterwards read a sort of satirical burlesque, called " Fanny," by Hallek: the wit being chiefly confined to local allusions and descriptions of New York manners, I could not derive much amusement from it. * * * *
* * * * *
* * * * *

When my father came home, went with him to call on Mrs. ———. What I saw of the house appeared to me very pretty, and well adapted to the heat of the season. A large and lofty room, paved with India matting, and furnished with white divans, and chairs, no other furniture encumbering or cramming it up; it looked very airy and cool. Our hostess did not put herself much out of the way to entertain us, but after the first " how do you do," continued conversing with another visiter, leaving us to the mercy of a very pretty young lady, who carried on the conversation at an average of a word every three minutes. Neither Mr. —— nor his eldest daughter were at home; the latter, however, presently came in, and relieved her sister and me greatly. We sat the proper time, and then came away.　　　　*　　　*

　　*　　　*　　　*　　　*　　　*

This is a species of intercourse I love not any where. I never practised it in my own blessed land, neither will I here. We dined at six : after dinner played and sang till eight, and then walked out with D—— and my father, by the most brilliant moonlight in the world. We went down to the Battery; the aquatic Vauxhall was lighted up very gaily, and they were sending up rockets every few minutes, which, shooting athwart the sky, threw a bright stream of light over the water, and falling back in showers of red stars, seemed to sink away before the steadfast shining of the moon, who held high supremacy in heaven. The bay lay like molten silver under her light, and every now and then a tiny skiff, emerging from the shade, crossed the bright waters, its dark hull and white sails relieved between the shining sea and radiant sky. Came home at nine, tea'd and sat embroidering till twelve o'clock, industrious little me.

Tuesday, 11th.

This day week we landed in New York; and this day was its prototype, rainy, dull, and dreary; with occasional fits of sunshine, and light delicious air, as capricious as a fine lady. After breakfast, Colonel —— called. Wrote journal, and practised till one o'clock. My father then set off with Colonel —— for Hoboken, 'a place across the water, famous once for duelling, but now the favourite resort of a turtle-eating club, who go there every Tuesday to cook and swallow turtle. The day was as bad as a party of pleasure could expect, (and when were their expectations of bad weather disappointed?) nathless, my father, at the Colonel's instigation, *persevered*, and went forth, leaving me his card of invitation, which

made me scream for half an hour; the wording
as follows: — " Sir, the Hoboken Turtle Club
will meet at the grove, for *spoon exercise*, on
Tuesday, the 11th inst., by order of the President." Mr. —— and the Doctor paid us a visit
of some length.   *   *   *   *

       *   *   *   *   *

When they were gone, read a canto in Dante,
and sketched till four o'clock. I wish I could
make myself draw. I want to do every thing in
the world that can be done, and, by the by, that
reminds me of my German, which I must *persecute*.
At four o'clock sent for a hair-dresser, that I
might in good time see that I am not made an
object on my first night. He was a Frenchman,
and after listening profoundly to my description
of the head-dress I wanted, replied, as none but
a Frenchman could, " *Madame, la difficulté n'est
pas d'exécuter votre coiffure mais de la bien con-
cevoir.*" However, he conceived and executed
sundry very smooth-looking bows, and, upon the
whole, dressed my hair very nicely, but charged a
dollar for so doing; O nefarious. D—— and I
dined *tête-à-tête;* the evening was sulky — I was
in miserable spirits.   *   *   *

       *   *   *   *   *

Sat working till my father came home, which
he did at about half past six. His account of his

dinner was any thing but delightful; to be sure
he has no taste for rainy ruralities, and his feeling
description of the damp ground, damp trees, damp
clothes, and damp atmosphere, gave me the
rheumatiz, letting alone that they had nothing to
eat but turtle, and that out of iron spoons,— " Ah,
you vill go a pleasuring."   *   *   *
    *   *   *   *   *

He had a cold before, and I fear this will make
him very ill. He went like wisdom to take a
vapour bath directly. —— came, and sat with
us till he returned. Had tea at eight, and embroidered till midnight. The wind is rioting over
the earth. I should like to see the Hudson now.
The black clouds, like masses of dark hair, are
driven over the moon's pale face, the red lights
and fire engines are dancing up and down the
streets, the church bells are all tolling — 't is sad
and strange.

> 'T is all in vain, it may not last,
> The sickly sunlight dies away,
> And the thick clouds that veil the past,
> Roll darkly o'er my present day.
>
> Have I not flung them off, and striven
> To seek some dawning hope in vain;
> Have I not been for ever driven
> Back to the bitter past again?

What though a brighter sky bends o'er
Scenes where no former image greets me,
Though lost in paths untrod before,
Here, even here, pale Memory meets me.

Oh life — oh blighted bloomless tree!
Why cling thy fibres to the earth?
Summer can bring no flower to thee,
Autumn no bearing, spring no birth.

Bid me not strive, I'll strive no more,
To win from pain my joyless breast;
Sorrow has ploughed too deeply o'er
Life's Eden — let it take the rest!

Wednesday, 12*th.*

Rose at eight.   After breakfast, heard my father
say Hamlet.   How beautiful his whole conception
of that part is, and yet it is but an actor's conception too.   *   *   *   *
            *   *   *   *   *
I am surprised at any body's ever questioning the
real madness of Hamlet: I know but one passage
in the play which tells against it, and there are a
thousand that go to prove it.   But leaving all
isolated parts out of the question, the entire colour
of the character is the proper ground from which
to draw the right deduction.   Gloomy, despond-

ing, ambitious, and disappointed in his ambition, full of sorrow for a dead father, of shame for a living mother, of indignation for his ill-filled inheritance, of impatience at his own dependent position; of a thoughtful, doubtful, questioning spirit, looking with timid boldness from the riddles of earth and life, to those of death and the mysterious land beyond it; weary of existence upon its very threshold, and withheld alone from self-destruction by religious awe, and that pervading uncertainty of mind which stands on the brink, brooding over the unseen may-be of another world; in love, moreover, and sad and dreamy in his affection, as in every other sentiment; for there is not enough of absolute passion in his love to make it a powerful and engrossing interest; had it been such, the entireness and truth of Hamlet's character would have been destroyed. 'T is love indeed, but a pulseless, powerless love; gentle, refined, and tender, but without ardour or energy; such are the various elements of Hamlet's character, at the very beginning of the play: then see what follows. A frightful and unnatural visitation from the dead; a horrible and sudden revelation of the murder of the father, for whom his soul is in mourning; thence burning hatred and thirst of vengeance against his uncle; double loathing of his mother's frailty; above all, that heaviest burden that a human creature can have put upon him, an imperative duty calling for fulfilment, and a want of resolution and activity to meet the demand; thence an unceasing struggle between the sluggish nature and the upbraiding soul; an eternal self-spurring and self-accusing, from which mental conflict, alone sufficient to unseat a stronger mind, he finds relief in fits of desponding musing, the exhaustion of overwrought powers. Then comes the vigilant and circumspect guard he is forced to keep upon every word, look, and action, lest they reveal his terrible secret; the suspicion and mistrust of all that surround him, authorised by his knowledge of his uncle's nature; his constant watchfulness over the spies that are set to watch him; then come, in the course of events, Polonius's death, the unintentional work of his own sword, the second apparition of his father's ghost, his banishment to England, still haunted by his treacherous friends, the miserable death of poor Ophelia, together with the unexpected manner of his first hearing of it — if all these — the man's own nature, sad and desponding — his educated nature (at a German university), reasoning and metaphysical — and the nature he acquires from the tutelage of events, bitter, dark, amazed, and uncertain ; if these do not make up as complete a madman as ever walked between heaven and earth, I know not what does.* Wrote journal, and began to practise ; while doing so, —— called ; he said that he was accompanied by some friends who wished to see me, and were at the door. I 've heard of men's shutting the door in the face of a dun, and going out the back way to escape a bailiff—but how to get rid of such an attack as this I knew not, and was therefore fain to beg the gentlemen would walk in, and accordingly in they walked, four as fine grown men as you would wish to see on a summer's day. I was introduced to this regiment man by man, and thought, as my Sheffield friend would say, " If *them* be American manners, defend me from them." They are traders, to be sure ; but I never heard of such wholesale introduction in my life. They sat a little while, behaved very

---

* I have lately read Goethe's Wilhelm Meister. In that wonderful analysis of the first work of our master-mind by his German peer, all has been said upon this subject that the most philosophical reason, or poetical imagination, can suggest ; and who that has read it can forget that most appropriate and beautiful simile, wherein Hamlet's mind is likened to an acorn planted in a porcelain vase — the seed becomes living — the roots expand — and the fragile vessel bursts into a thousand shivers.

like Christians, and then departed. Captain —— and —— called, — the former to ask us to come down and see the Pacific, poor old lady! When they were gone, practised, read a canto in Dante, and translated verbatim a German fable, which kept me till dinner-time. After dinner, walked out towards the Battery. —— joined us. It was between sunset and moonrise, and a lovelier light never lay upon sea, earth, and sky. The horizon was bright orange colour, fading as it rose to pale amber, which died away again into the modest violet colour of twilight; this possessed the main sky wholly, except where two or three masses of soft dark purple clouds floated, from behind which the stars presently winked at us with their bright eyes. The river lay as still as death, though there was a delicious fresh air: tiny boats were stealing like shadows over the water; and every now and then against the orange edge of the sky moved the masts of some schooner, whose hull was hidden in the deep shadow thrown over it by the Jersey coast. A band was playing in the Castle garden, and not a creature but ourselves seemed abroad to see all this loveliness. Fashion makes the same fools all the world over; and Broadway, with its crowded dusty pavement, and in the full glare of day, is preferable, in the eyes of the New York promenaders, to this cool and beautiful walk. Came home at about nine. On the stairs met that odious Dr. ——, who came into the drawing-room without asking or being asked, sat himself down, and called me " Miss Fanny." I should like to have thrown my tea at him ! —— sent up his name and presently followed it. I like to see any of our fellow-pas-sengers, however little such society would have pleased me under any other circumstances ; but necessity " makes us acquainted with strange bed-fellows ; " and these my ship-mates will, to the end of time, be my very good friends and boon com-panions. My father went to the Park theatre, to see a man of the name of Hacket give an Ameri-can entertainment after Matthews's at-home fashion. I would not go, but staid at home looking at the moon, which was glorious. * * *

* * * * *

* * * * *

To-night, as I stood watching that surpassing sunset, I would have given it all — gold, and purple, and all — for a wreath of English fog stealing over the water.

Thursday, 13*th.*

Rose late : there was music in the night, which is always a strange enchantment to me. After breakfast, wrote journal. At eleven, Captain —— and —— called for us; and my uncle having joined us, we proceeded to the slip, as they call the places where the ships lie, and which answer to our docks. Poor dear Pacific ! I ran up her side with great glee, and was introduced to Captain ——, her old commander; rushed down into my berth, and was actually growing pathetic over the scene of my sea-sorrows, when Mr. —— clapped his hands close to me, and startled me out of my reverie. Certainly my *adhesiveness* must either be very large, or uncommonly active just now, for my heart yearned towards the old timbers with exceeding affection. The old ship was all drest out in her best, and after sitting for some time in our cabin, we adjourned to the larger one and lunched. Mr. —— joined our party; and we had one or two of our old ship songs, with their ridiculous burdens, with due solemnity. Saw Mr. ——, but not dear M. ——. Visited the forecastle, whence I have watched such glorious sunsets, such fair uprisings of the starry sisterhood; now it looked upon the dusty quay and dirty dock water, and the graceful sails were all stripped away, and the bare masts and rigging shone in the intense sunlight. Poor good ship, I wish to Heaven my feet were on her deck, and her prow turned to the east. I would not care if the devil himself drove a hurricane at our backs. Visited the fish and fruit markets *: it was too late in the day to see either to advantage, but the latter reminded me of Aladdin's treasure: the heaps of peaches, filling with their rich downy balls high baskets ranged in endless rows, and painted of a bright vermilion colour, which threw a ruddy ripeness over the fruit. The enormous baskets (such as are used in England to carry linen) piled with melons, the wild grapes, the pears and apples, all so plenteous, so fragrant,

* The fish of these waters may be excellent in the water; but owing to the want of care and niceness with which they are kept after being caught, they are very seldom worth eating when brought to table. They have no turbot or soles, a great national misfortune: their best fish are rock-fish, bass, shad, (an excellent herring, as big as a small salmon,) and sheep's head. Cod and salmon I have eaten; but from the above cause they were never comparable to the same fish at an English table. The lobsters, crabs, and oysters are all gigantic, frightful to behold, and not particularly well-flavoured: their size makes them tough and coarse.

so beautiful in form and colour, leading the mind
to the wondrous bounteousness which has dowered
this land with every natural treasure — the whole
enchanted me. ——, to my horror, bought a
couple of beautiful live wild-pigeons, which he
carried home, head downwards, one in each coat
pocket. We parted from him at the park gate,
and proceeded to Murray Street, to look at the
furnished house my father wishes to take. Upon
enquiry, however, we found that it was already
let. The day was bright and beautiful, and
my father proposed crossing the river to Hoboken, the scene of the turtle-eating expedition.
We did so accordingly: himself, D——, Mr.
——, and I. Steamers go across every five
minutes, conveying passengers on foot and horseback, gigs, carriages, carts, any thing and every
thing. The day was lovely — the broad, bright
river was gemmed with a thousand sails. Away
to the right it stretched between richly wooded
banks, placid and blue as a lake; to the left, in
the rocky doorway of the narrows, two or three
ships stood revealed against the cloudless sky.
We reached the opposite coast, and walked. It
was nearly three miles from where we landed to
the scene of the " *spoon-exercise.*" The whole of
our route lay through a beautiful wild plantation,

or rather strip of wood, I should say, for 't is nature's own gardening which crowns the high bank of the river; through which trellice-work of varied foliage, we caught exquisite glimpses of the glorious waters, the glittering city, and the opposite banks, decked out in all the loveliest contrast of sunshine and shade. As we stood in our leafy colonnade looking out upon this fair scene, the rippling water made sweet music far down below us, striking with its tiny silver waves the smooth sand and dark-coloured rocks from which they were ebbing. Many of the trees were quite new to me, and delighted me with their graceful forms and vivid foliage. The broad-leaved catalpa, and the hickory with its bright coral-coloured berries. Many lovely, lowly things, too, grew by our pathside, which we gathered as we passed, to bring away, but which withered in our hands ere we returned. Gorgeous butterflies were zig-zagging through the air, and for the first time I longed to imprison them. In pursuing one, I ran into the midst of a slip of clover land, but presently jumped out again, on hearing the swarms of grasshoppers round me. Mr. —— caught one; it was larger and thicker than the English grasshopper, and of a dim mottled brown colour, like the plumage of our common moth; but presently

on his opening his hand to let it escape, it spread
out a pair of dark purple wings, tipped with pale
primrose colour, and flew away a beautiful but-
terfly, such as the one I had been seduced by.
The slips of grass ground on the left of our path
were the only things that annoyed me: they were
ragged, and rank, and high, — they wanted mow-
ing; and if they had been mowed soft, and thick,
and smooth, like an English lawn, how gloriously
the lights and shadows of this lovely sky would
fall through the green roof of this wood upon
them. There is nothing in nature that, to my
fancy, receives light and shade with as rich an
effect as sloping lawn land. Oh! England,
England! how I have seen your fresh emerald
mantle deepen and brighten in a summer's day.
About a hundred yards from the place where they
dined on Tuesday, with no floor but the damp
earth, no roof but the dripping trees, stands a sort
of *café;* a long, low, pretty Italianish-looking
building. The wood is cleared away in front of
it, and it commands a lovely view of the Hudson
and its opposite shores: and here they might
have been sheltered and comfortable, but I suppose it was not yet the appointed day of the
month with them for eating their dinner within
walls; and, rather than infringe on an established

rule, they preferred catching a cold apiece. The place where they met in the open air is extremely beautiful, except, of course, on a rainy day. The shore is lower just here; and though there are trees enough to make shade all round, and a thick screen of wood and young undergrowth behind, the front is open to the river, which makes a bend just below, forming a lake-like bay, round which again the coast rises into rocky walls covered with rich foliage. Upon one of these promontories, in the midst of a high, open knoll, surrounded and overhung by higher grounds covered with wood, stood the dwelling of the owner of the land, high above the river, overlooking its downward course to the sea, perched like an eagle's aërie, half-way between heaven and the level earth, but beautifully encircled with waving forests, a shade in summer and a shelter in winter. My father, D——, and my bonnet sat down in the shade. Mr. —— and I clambered upon some pieces of rock at the water's edge, whence we looked out over river and land — a fair sight. "Oh!" I exclaimed, pointing to the highlands on our left, through whose rich foliage the rifted granite looked cold and grey, "what a place for a scramble! there must be lovely walks there." "Ay," returned my companion, "and a few rattle-snakes too." * We found D——, my father, and my bonnet buffeting with a swarm of musquitoes; this is a great nuisance. We turned our steps homeward. I picked up a nut enclosed like a walnut in a green case. I opened it; it was not ripe; but in construction exactly like a walnut, with the same bitter filmy skin over the fruit, which is sweet and oily, and like a walnut in flavour also. Mr. —— told me it was called a marrow-nut. The tree on which it grew had foliage of the acacia kind. We had to rush to meet the steam-boat, which was just going across: the whole walk reminded me of that part of Oattands which, from its wild and tangled wood-land, they call America.   *   *   *

*   *   *   *   *

There must have been something surpassingly beautiful in our surroundings, for even Mr. ——, into whose composition I suspect much of the poetical element does not enter, began expatiating on the happiness of the original possessors of these fair lands and waters, the Indians — the Red

* My friend was entertaining himself, at the expense of my credulity, in making this assertion. The rattle-snakes and red Indians have fled together before the approach of civilisation; and it would be as difficult to find the one as the other in the vicinity of any of the large cities of the northern states.

Children of the soil, who followed the chase through these lovely wildernesses, and drove their light canoes over these broad streams — " great nature's happy commoners," — till the predestined curse came on them, till the white sails of the invaders threw their shadow over these seas, and the work of extermination began in these wild fastnesses of freedom. The destruction of the original inhabitants of a country by its discoverers, always attended, as it is, with injustice and cruelty, appears to me one of the most mysterious dispensations of Providence.

The chasing, enslaving, and destroying creatures, whose existence, however inferior, is as justly theirs, as that of the most refined European is his; who, for the most part, too, receive their enemies with open-handed hospitality, until taught treachery by being betrayed, and cruelty by fear; the driving the child of the soil off it, or, what is fifty times worse, chaining him to till it; all the various forms of desolation which have ever followed the landing of civilised men upon uncivilised shores; in short, the theory and practice of discovery and conquest, as recorded in all history, is a very singular and painful subject of contemplation.

'T is true that cultivation and civilisation, the

arts and sciences that render life useful, the knowledge that ennobles, the adornments that refine
existence, above all, the religion that is the most
sacred trust and dear reward, all these, like pure
sunshine and healthful airs following a hurricane,
succeed the devastation of the invader; but the
sufferings of those who are swept away are not
the less; and though I believe that good alone is
God's result, it seems a fearful proof of the evil
wherewith this earth is cursed, that good cannot
progress but over such a path. No one, beholding
the prosperous and promising state of this fine
country, could wish it again untenanted of its
enterprising and industrious possessors; yet even
while looking with admiration at all that they
have achieved, with expectation amounting to certainty to all that they will yet accomplish, 't is
difficult to refrain from bestowing some thoughts
of pity and of sadness upon those whose homes
have been overturned, whose language has passed
away, and whose feet are daily driven further from
those territories of which they were once sole and
sovereign lords. How strange it is to think, that
less than one hundred years ago, these shores,
resounding with the voice of populous cities, —
these waters, laden with the commerce of the wide
world, — were silent wildernesses, where sprang and

fell the forest leaves, where ebbed and flowed the
ocean tides from day to day, and from year to
year in uninterrupted stillness; where the great
sun, who looked on the vast empires of the East,
its mouldering kingdoms, its lordly palaces, its
ancient temples, its swarming cities, came and
looked down upon the still dwelling of utter lone-
liness, where nature sat enthroned in everlasting
beauty, undisturbed by the far-off din of worlds
" beyond the flood." *

* It is two years since I visited Hoboken for the first
time; it is now more beautiful than ever. The good taste
of the proprietor has made it one of the most picturesque
and delightful places imaginable; it wants but a good carriage-road along the water's edge (for which the ground lies
very favourably) to make it as perfect a public promenade
as any European city can boast, with the advantage of such a
river, for its principal object, as none of them possess.

I think the European traveller, in order to form a just
estimate both of the evils and advantages deriving from the
institutions of this country, should spend one day in the
streets of New York, and the next in the walks of Hoboken.
If in the one, the toil, the care, the labour of mind and body,
the outward and visible signs of the debasing pursuit of
wealth, are marked in melancholy characters upon every man
he meets, and bear witness to the great curse of the country;
in the other, the crowds of happy, cheerful, enjoying beings
of that order, which, in the old world, are condemned to
ceaseless and ill-requited labour, will testify to the blessings
which counterbalance that curse. I never was so forcibly
struck with the prosperity and happiness of the lower orders

Came home rather tired: my father asked Mr. —— to dine with us, but he could not. After

---

of society in this country as yesterday returning from Hoboken. The walks along the river and through the woods, the steamers crossing from the city, were absolutely thronged with a cheerful, well-dressed population abroad, merely for the purpose of pleasure and exercise. Journeymen, labourers, handicraftsmen, trades-people, with their families, bearing all in their dress and looks evident signs of well-being and contentment, were all flocking from their confined avocations, into the pure air, the bright sunshine, and beautiful shade of this lovely place. I do not know any spectacle which could give a foreigner, especially an Englishman, a better illustration of that peculiar excellence of the American government — the freedom and happiness of the lower classes. Neither is it to be said that this was a holyday, or an occasion of peculiar festivity — it was a common week-day — such as our miserable manufacturing population spends from sun-rise to sun-down, in confined, incessant, unhealthy toil — to earn, at its conclusion, the inadequate reward of health and happiness so wasted. The contrast struck me forcibly — it rejoiced my heart; it surely was an object of contemplation, that any one who had a heart must have rejoiced in. Presently, however, came the following reflections : —, These people are happy — their wants are satisfied, their desires fulfilled — their capacities of enjoyment meet with full employment — they are well fed — well clothed — well housed — moderate labour insures them all this, and leaves them leisure for such recreations as they are capable of enjoying; but how is it with me ? — and I mean not *me myself* alone, but all who, like myself, have received a higher degree of mental cultivation, whose estimate of happiness is, therefore, so much higher, whose capacity for enjoyment is so much more expanded and

dinner, sat working till ten o'clock, when ——
came to take leave of us. He is going off to-
morrow morning to Philadelphia, but will be back
for our Tuesday's dinner. The people here are
all up and about very early in the morning. I went
out at half-past eight, and found all Broadway
abroad.

---

cultivated; — can I be satisfied with a race in a circular rail-
road car, or a swing between the lime-trees? where are my
peculiar objects of pleasure and recreation? where are the
picture-galleries — the sculptures — the works of art and
science — the countless wonders of human ingenuity and
skill — the cultivated and refined society — the intercourse
with men of genius, literature, scientific knowledge — where
are all the sources from which I am to draw my recreations?
They are not. The heart of a philanthropist may indeed be
satisfied, but the intellectual man feels a dearth that is inex-
pressibly painful; and in spite of the real and great pleasure
which I derived from the sight of so much enjoyment, I
could not help desiring that enjoyment of another order were
combined with it. Perhaps the two are incompatible; if so,
I would not alter the present state of things if I could.

The losers here are decidedly in the minority. Indeed, so
much so, as hardly to form a class; they are a few individuals,
scattered over the country, and of course their happiness
ought not to come into competition with that of the mass of
the people; but the Americans, at the same time that they
make no provision whatever for the happiness of such a portion of their inhabitants, would be very angry if one were to
say it was a very inconsiderable one, and yet that is the
truth.

Friday, 14*th.*

Forget all about it, except that I went about the town with Colonel ——.   *   *   *

    *   *   *   *   *

went to see his Quaker wife, whom I liked very much.   *   *   *   *   *

    *   *   *   *   *

Drove all about New York, which more than ever reminded me of the towns in France : passed the Bowery theatre, which is a handsome, finely-proportioned building, with a large brazen eagle plastered on the pediment, for all the world like an insurance mark, or the sign of the spread eagle : this is nefarious ! We passed a pretty house, which Colonel —— called an old mansion ; mercy on me, him, and it ! Old ! I thought of Warwick Castle, of Hatfield, of Checquers, of Hopwood, — old, and there it stood, with its white pillars and Italian-looking portico, for all the world like one of our own cit's yesterday-grown boxes. Old, quotha ! the woods and waters, and hills and skies alone are old here ; the works of men are in the very greenness and unmellowed imperfection of youth; true, 'tis a youth full of vigorous sap and glorious promise; spring, laden with blossoms, foretelling abundant and rich produce, and so let them be proud of it. But the worst of it is, the Americans are not satisfied with glorying in what they are, — which, considering the time and opportunities they have had, is matter of glory quite sufficient, — they are never happy without comparing this their sapling to the giant oaks of the old world, — and what can one say to that? *Is* New York like London? No, by my two troths it is not; but the oak was an acorn once, and New York will surely, if the world holds together long enough, become a lordly city, such as we know of beyond the sea.

Went in the evening to see Wallack act the Brigand; it was his benefit, and the house was very good. He is perfection in this sort of thing, yet there were one or two blunders even in his melo-dramatic acting of this piece; however, he looks very like the thing, and it is very nice to see — once.

Saturday, 15*th.*

Sat stitching all the blessed day. So we are to go to *Philadelphia* before *Boston.* I'm sorry. The H———s will be disappointed, and I shall get no riding, *che seccatura!* At five dressed, and

went to the ——, where we were to dine. This is
one of the first houses here, so I conclude that
I am to consider what I see as a tolerable sample
of the ways and manners of being, doing, and suffering of the *best society* in New York. There
were about twenty people ; the women were in a
sort of French demi-toilette, with bare necks, and
long sleeves, heads frizzed out after the very last
petit courier, and thread net handkerchiefs and
capes ; the whole of which, to my English eye,
appeared a strange marrying of incongruities.
The younger daughter of our host is beautiful ; a
young and brilliant likeness of Ellen Tree, with
more refinement, and a smile that was, not to say
a ray, but a whole focus of sun rays, a perfect
blaze of light ; she was much taken up with a
youth, to whom, my neighbour at dinner informed
me, she was engaged.   *   *   *

*   *   *   *   *

The women here, like those of most warm climates,
ripen very early, and decay proportionably soon.
They are, generally speaking, pretty, with good
complexions, and an air of freshness and brilliancy, but this, I am told, is very evanescent ; and
whereas, in England,.a woman is in the full bloom
of health and beauty from twenty to five-and-
thirty, here they scarcely reach the first period

without being faded and looking old.* They marry very young, and this is another reason why age comes prematurely upon them. There was a fair young thing at dinner to-day, who did not look above seventeen, and she was a wife. As for their figures, like those of French women, they are too well dressed for one to judge exactly what they are really like: they are, for the most part, short and slight, with remarkably pretty feet and ankles; but there's too much pelerine and petticoat, and "de quoi" of every sort to guess any thing more. * * * *

   *   *   *   *   *

   *   *   *   *   *

There was a Mr. ——, the magnus Apollo of New York, who is a musical genius : sings as well as any gentleman need sing, pronounces Italian well, and accompanies himself without false chords; all which renders him *the* man round whom (as round H——, G——, Lord C——, and that pretty Lord O——, in our own country,)

* The climate of this country is the scape-goat upon which all the ill looks and ill health of the ladies is laid; but while they are brought up as effeminately as they are, take as little exercise, live in rooms like ovens during the winter, and marry as early as they do, it will appear evident that many causes combine with an extremely variable climate, to sallow their complexions, and destroy their constitutions.

the women listen and languish. He sang the
Phantom Bark: the last time I heard it was from
the lips of Moore, with two of the loveliest faces
in all the world hanging over him, Mrs. N——,
and Mrs. B——. By the by, the man who sat
next me at dinner was asking me all manner of
questions about Mrs. N——; among others, whether she was " as pale as a poetess ought to be !"
Oh ! how I wish Corinne had but heard that
herself! what a deal of funny scorn would have
looked beautiful on her rich brown cheek and
brilliant lips. The dinner was plenteous, and
tolerably well dressed, but ill served : there were
not half servants enough, and we had neither
water-glasses nor finger-glasses. Now, though I
don't eat with my fingers, (except peaches, whereat
I think the aborigines, who were paring theirs
like so many potatoes, seemed rather amazed,) yet
do I hold a finger-glass at the conclusion of my
dinner a requisite to comfort. After dinner we
had coffee, but no tea, whereat my English taste
was in high dudgeon. The gentlemen did not
sit long, and when they joined us, Mr. ——, as I
said before, uttered sweet sounds. By the by, I
was not a little amused at Mrs. —— asking me
whether I had heard of his singing, or their
musical soirees, and seeming all but surprised that

I had no revelations of either across the Atlantic. Mercy on me! what fools people are all over the world! The worst is, they are all fools of the same sort, and there is no profit whatever in travelling. Mr. B——, who is an Englishman, happened to ask me if I knew Captain ——, whereupon we immediately struck up a conversation, and talked over English folks and doings together, to my entire satisfaction. The —— were there: he is brother to that wondrous ruler of the spirits whom I did so dislike in London, and his lady is a daughter of Lord ——.   *

*   *   *   *   *

*   *   *   *   *

I was very glad to come home. I sang to them two or three things, but the piano was pitched too high for my voice; by the by, in that large, lofty, fine room, they had a tiny, old-fashioned, be-curtained cabinet piano stuck right against the wall, unto which the singer's face was turned, and into which his voice was absorbed. We had hardly regained our inn and uncloaked, when there came a tap at the door, and in walked Mr. —— to ask me if we would not join them (himself and the ——) at supper. He said that, besides five being a great deal too early to dine, he had not half dinner enough; and then began the regular English quizzing of every thing and every body we had left behind. Oh dear, oh dear! how thoroughly English it was, and how it reminded me of H——; of course, we did not accept their invitation, but it furnished me matter of amusement. How we English folks do cling to our own habits, our own views, our own things, our own people; how, in spite of all our wanderings and scatterings over the whole face of the earth, like so many Jews, we never lose our distinct and national individuality; nor fail to lay hold of one another's skirts, to laugh at and depreciate all that differs from that country, which we delight in forsaking for any and all others.

Sunday, 16*th.*

Rose at eight. After breakfast, walked to church with the C——s and Mr. B——. They went to Grace church for the music; we stopped short to go to the —— pew in the Episcopal church. The pew was crammed, I am sorry to say, owing to our being there, which they had pressed so earnestly, that we thought ourselves bound to accept the invitation. The sermon was tolerably good; better than the average sermons one hears in London, and sufficiently well delivered. After church,

I—— called, also two men of the name of M——, large men, very! also Mr. B—— and Mr. C——: when they were all gone, wrote journal, and began a letter to J——. Dined at five; after dinner, went on with my letter to J——, and wrote an immense one to dear H——, which kept me pen in hand till past twelve. A tremendous thunder-storm came on, which lasted from nine o'clock till past two in the morning: I never saw but one such in my life; and that was our memorable Weybridge storm, which only exceeded this in the circumstance of my having seen a thunderbolt fall during that paroxysm of the elements. But this was very glorious, awful, beautiful, and tremendous. The lightning played without the intermission of a second, in wide sheets of purple glaring flame that trembled over the earth for nearly two or three seconds at a time; making the whole world, river, sky, trees, and buildings, look like a ghostly universe cut out in chalk. The light over the water, which absolutely illumined the shore on the other side with the broad glare of full day, was of a magnificent purple colour. The night was pitchy dark, too; so that between each of these ghastly smiles of the devil, the various pale steeples and buildings, which seemed at every moment to leap from nothing into existence, after standing out in

fearful relief against a back-ground of fire, were
hidden like so many dreams in deep and total
darkness.   God's music rolled along the heavens;
the forked lightnings now dived from the clouds
into the very bosom of the city, now ran like
tangled threads of fire all round the blazing sky.
" The big bright rain came dancing to the earth,"
the wind clapped its huge wings, and swept through
the dazzling glare; and as I stood, with eyes half
veiled (for the light was too intense even upon the
ground to be looked at with unshaded eyes),
gazing at this fierce holyday of the elements — at
the mad lightning — at the brilliant shower, through
which the flashes shone like daylight—listening to
the huge thunder, as its voice resounded, and its
heavy feet rebounded along the clouds—and the
swift spirit-like wind rushing triumphantly along,
uttering its wild pæan over the amazed earth;—
I felt more intensely than I ever did before
the wondrous might of these, God's powerful
and beautiful creatures; the wondrous might,
majesty, and awfulness of him their Lord, beneath
whose footstool they lie chained, by his great goodness made the ministers of good to this our lowly
dwelling-place.   I did not go to bed till two; the
storm continued to rage long after that.

Monday, 17*th.*

Rose at eight. At twelve, went to rehearsal. The weather is intolerable; I am in a state of perpetual fusion. The theatre is the coolest place I have yet been in, I mean at rehearsal; when the front is empty, and the doors open, and the stage is so dark that we are obliged to rehearse by candlelight. That washed-out man who failed in London when he acted Romeo with me is to be my Fazio; let us hope he will know some of his words to-morrow night, for he is at present most innocent of any such knowledge. After rehearsal, walked into a shop to buy some gauze: the shopman called me by my name, entered into conversation with us; and one of them, after showing me a variety of things which I did not want, said, that they were most anxious to show me every attention, and render my stay in this country agreeable. A Christian, I suppose, would have met these benevolent advances with an infinitude of thankfulness, and an outpouring of grateful pleasure; but for my own part, though I had the grace to smile and say, " Thank you," I longed to add, " but be so good as to measure your ribands, and hold your tongue." I have no idea of holding parley with

clerks behind a counter, still less of their doing so
with me. So much for my first impression of the
courtesy of this land of liberty. I should have
been much better pleased if they had called me
" Ma'am," which they did not. We dined at
three. V—— and Colonel —— called after
dinner. At seven, went to the theatre. It was my
dear father's first appearance in this new world,
and my heart ached with anxiety. The weather
was intensely hot, yet the theatre was crowded :
when he came on, they gave him what every body
here calls an immense reception ; but they should
see our London audience get up, and wave hats
and handkerchiefs, and shout welcome as they do
to us. The tears were in my eyes, and all I could
say was, " They might as well get up, I think."
My father looked well, and acted beyond all praise ;
but oh, what a fine and delicate piece of work this
is ! There is not one sentence, line, or word of this
part which my father has not sifted grain by grain ;
there is not one scene or passage to which he does
not give its fullest and most entire substance, together with a variety that relieves the intense study
of the whole with wonderful effect.   *   *

  *   *   *   *   *

  *   *   *   *   *

I think that it is impossible to conceive Hamlet

more truly, or execute it more exquisitely than he does. The refinement, the tenderness, the grace, dignity, and princely courtesy with which he invests it from beginning to end, are most lovely; and some of the slighter passages, which, like fine tints to the incapable eyes of blindness, must always pass unnoticed, and, of course, utterly uncomprehended, by the discriminating public, enchanted me.   *   *   *

    *   *   *   *   *

    *   *   *   *   *

His voice was weak from nervousness and the intolerable heat of the weather, and he was not well dressed, which was a pity.   *   *

    *   *   *   *   *

    *   *   *   *   *

The play was well got up, and went off very well. The —— were there, a regiment of them; also Colonel —— and Captain ——. After the play, came home to supper.

Tuesday, 18*th.*

Rose at eight. At eleven, went to rehearsal. Mr. Keppel is just as nervous and as imperfect as ever: what on earth will he, or shall I, do to-night! Came home, got things out for the

theatre, and sat like any stroller stitching for dear
life at my head-dress.   Mr. H—— and his nephew called: the latter asked me if I was at all
apprehensive? No, by my troth, I am not; and
that not because I feel sure of success, for I
think it very probable the Yankees may like to
show their critical judgment and independence by
damning me; but because, thank God, I do not
care whether they do or not: the whole thing is
too loathsome to me, for either failure or success
to affect me in the least, and therefore I feel neither nervous nor anxious about it.   We dined at
three: after dinner, J—— came; he sat some
time.   When he was gone, I came into the drawing-room, and found a man sitting with my father,
who presented him to me by some inaudible name.
I sat down, and the gentleman pursued his conversation as follows:—" When Clara Fisher came
over, Barry wrote to me about her, and I wrote
him back word: ' My dear fellow, if your bella
donna is such as you describe, why, we 'll see what
we can do; we will take her by the hand.' "   This
was enough for me.   I jumped up, and ran out of
the room; because a newspaper writer is my aversion.   At half-past six, went to the theatre. They
acted the farce of Popping the Question first, in
order, I suppose, to get the people to their places

before the play began. Poor Mr. Keppel was gasping for breath; he moved my compassion infinitely; I consoled and comforted him all I could, gave him some of my lemonade to swallow, for he was choking with fright; sat myself down with my back to the audience, and up went the curtain. Owing to the position in which I was sitting, and my plain dress, most unheroine-like in its make and colour, the people did not know me, and would not have known me for some time, if that stupid man had done as I kept bidding him, gone on; but instead of doing so, he stood stock still, looked at me, and then at the audience, whereupon the latter caught an inkling of the truth, and gave me such a reception as I get in Covent Garden theatre every time I act a new part. The house was very full; all the —— were there, and Colonel ——. Mr. Keppel was frightened to death, and in the very second speech was quite out: it was in vain that I prompted him; he was too nervous to take the word, and made a complete mess of it. This happened more than once in the first scene; and at the end of the first act, as I left the stage, I said to D——, " It's all up with me, I can't do any thing now;" for having to prompt my Fazio, frightened by his fright, annoyed by his forgetting his crossings and positions, utterly unable to work myself into any thing like excitement, I thought the whole thing must necessarily go to pieces. However, once rid of my encumbrance, which I am at the end of the second act, I began to move a little more freely, gathered up my strength, and set to work comfortably by myself; whereupon, the people applauded, I warmed, (warmed, quotha? the air was steam,) and got through very satisfactorily, at least so it seems. My dresses were very beautiful; but oh, but oh, the musquitoes had made dreadful havoc with my arms, which were covered with hills as large and red as Vesuvius in an eruption. After the play, my father introduced me to Mr. B——, Lord S——'s brother, who was behind the scenes; his brother's place, by the by. Came home, supped.   *   *   *   *

    *   *   *   *   *

    *   *   *   *   *

Came to bed at half past twelve; weary, and half melted away. The ants swarm on the floors, on the tables, in the beds, about one's clothes; the plagues of Egypt were a joke to them: horrible! it makes one's life absolutely burdensome, to have creatures creeping about one, and all over one, night and day, this fashion; to say nothing of those cantankerous stinging things, the musquitoes.

Wednesday 19th.

D—— did not call me till ten o'clock, whereat I was in furious dudgeon. Got up, breakfasted, and off to rehearsal; Romeo and Juliet. Mr. Keppel has been dismissed, poor man! I'm sorry for him: my father is to play Romeo with me, I'm sorrier still for that. After rehearsal, came home, dawdled about my room: Mr. —— called: he is particularly fond of music. My father asked him to try the piano, which he accordingly did, and was playing most delightfully, when in walked Mr. ——, and by and by Colonel ——, with his honour the Recorder, and General —— of the militia. I amused myself with looking over some exquisite brown silk stockings, wherewith I mean to match my gown. When they were all gone, dawdled about till time to dress. So poor dear H—— can't come from Philadelphia for our dinner — dear, I'm quite sorry! At five our party assembled: we were but thin in numbers, and the half empty table, together with the old ship faces, made it look, as some one observed, as if it was blowing hard. Our dinner was neither good nor well served, the wine not half iced. At the end of it, my father gave Captain —— his claret jug, wherewith that worthy seemed much satisfied.   *   *

*   *   *   *   *

We left the table soon; came and wrote journal. When the gentlemen joined us, they were all more or less " how com'd you so indeed?" Mr. —— and Mr. ―— particularly. They put me down to the piano, and once or twice I thought I must have screamed. On one side *vibrated* dear Mr. ——, threatening my new gown with a cup of coffee, which he held at an awful angle from the horizontal line; singing with every body who opened their lips, and uttering such dreadfully discordant little squeals and squeaks, that I thought I should have died of suppressed laughter. On the other side, rather *concerned*, but not quite so much so, stood the Irishman; who, though warbling a little out of tune, and flourishing somewhat luxuriantly, still retained enough of his right senses to discriminate between Mr. ——'s yelps and singing, properly so called; and accordingly pished! — and pshawed! — and oh Lorded! — and good heavened! away, — staring at the perpetrator with indignant horror through his spectacles, while his terrified wig stood on end in every direction, each particular hair appearing vehemently possessed with the centrifugal force. They all went away in good time, and we came to bed.

—— To bed — to sleep —
To sleep!—perchance to be bitten! ay — there's the scratch :
And in that sleep of ours what bugs may come,
Must give us pause.

Thursday, 20th.

Rose at eight. After breakfast, went to rehearse Romeo and Juliet. Poor Mr. Keppel is fairly laid on the shelf; I'm sorry for him! What a funny passion he had, by the by, for going down upon his knees. In Fazio, at the end of the judgment scene, when I was upon mine, down he went upon his, making the most absurd, devout looking *vis-à-vis* I ever beheld: in the last scene, too, when he ought to have been going off to execution, down he went again upon his knees, and no power on earth could get him up again, for Lord knows how long. Poor fellow, he bothered me a good deal, yet I'm sincerely sorry for him. At the end of our rehearsal, came home. The weather is sunny, sultry, scorching, suffocating. Ah! Mr. —— called. This is an indifferent imitation of bad fine manners amongst us; " he speaks small, too, like a gentleman." He sat for a long time, talking over the opera, and all the prima donnas in the world. When he was gone, Mr. —— and Mr. —— called.   *
   *   *   *   *   *

The latter asked us to dinner to-morrow, to meet
Dr. ——, who, poor man, dares neither go to the
play nor call upon us, so strict are the good people
here about the behaviour of their pastors and
masters. By the by, Essex called this morning
to fetch away the Captain's claret jug: he asked
my father for an order ; adding, with some hesitation, " It must be for the gallery, if you please,
sir, for people of colour are not allowed to go to
the pit, or any other part of the house." I believe
I turned black myself, I was so indignant. Here 's
aristocracy with a vengeance ! —— called with
Forrest, the American actor. Mr. Forrest has
rather a fine face, I think. We dined at three :
after dinner, wrote journal, played on the piano,
and frittered away my time till half-past six.
Went to the theatre : the house was very full,
and dreadfully hot. My father acted Romeo
beautifully : I looked very nice, and the people
applauded my *gown* abundantly. At the end of
the play I was half dead with heat and fatigue :
came home and supped, lay down on the floor in
absolute meltiness away, and then came to bed.

Friday, 21st.

Rose at eight. After breakfast went to rehearsal. The School for Scandal; Sir Peter, I
see, keeps his effects to himself; what a bore this
is, to be sure! Got out things for the theatre.
While eating my lunch, Mr. —— and his cousin,
a Mr. —— (one of the cleverest lawyers here),
called   *   *   *   *
   *   *   *   *   *
   *   *   *   *   *

They were talking of Mr. Keppel. By the by,
of that gentleman; Mr. Simpson sent me this
morning, for my decision, a letter from Mr. Keppel,
soliciting another trial, and urging the hardness
of his case, in being condemned upon a part
which he had had no time to study. My own
opinion of poor Mr. Keppel is, that no power on
earth or in heaven can make him act decently;
however, of course, I did not object to his trying
again; he did not swamp me the first night, so I
don't suppose he will the fifth. We dined at
five. Just before dinner, received a most delicious
bouquet, which gladdened my very heart with its
sweet smell and lovely colours: some of the
flowers were strangers to me. After dinner,

Colonel —— called, and began pulling out heaps of newspapers, and telling us a long story about Mr. Keppel, who, it seems, has been writing to the papers, to convince them and the public that he is a good actor, at the same time throwing out sundry hints, which seem aimed our way, of injustice, oppression, hard usage, and the rest on 't.

*   *   *   *   *

*   *   *   *   *

Mr. —— called to offer to ride with me; when, however, the question of a horse was canvassed, he knew of none, and Colonel ——'s whole regiment of " beautiful ladies' horses" had also neither a local habitation nor a name.   *

*   *   *   *   *

*   *   *   *   *

When they were gone, went to the theatre; the house was very good, the play, the School for Scandal. I played pretty fairly, and looked very nice. The people were stupid to a degree, to be sure; poor things! it was very hot. Indeed, I scarce understand how they should be amused with the School for Scandal; for though the dramatic situations are so exquisite, yet the wit is far above the generality of even our own audiences, and the tone and manners altogether are so thoroughly English, that I should think it must be for

the most part incomprehensible to the good people
here. After the play, came home. Colonel S——
supped with us, and renewed the subject of Mr.
Keppel and the theatre. My father happened
to say, referring to a passage in that worthy's letter
to the public, " I shall certainly enquire of Mr.
Keppel why he has so used my name ;" to which
Colonel S—— replied, as usual, " No, now let
me advise, let me beg you, Mr. Kemble, just to
remain quiet, and leave all this to me." This was
too much for mortal woman to bear. I immediately said, " Not at all : it is my father's affair,
if any body's ; and he alone has the right to
demand any explanation, or make any observation
on the subject; and were I he, I certainly should
do so, and that forthwith." I could hold no
longer.   *   *   *   *
            *   *   *   *   *
            *   *   *   *   *

Came to bed in tremendous dudgeon. The few
critiques that I have seen upon our acting, have
been, upon the whole, laudatory. One was sent
to me from a paper called The Mirror, which
pleased me very much ; not because the praise in
it was excessive, and far beyond my deserts, but
that it was written with great taste and feeling,
and was evidently not the produce of a common

press hack. There appeared to me in all the others the true provincial dread of praising too much, and being *led* into approbation by previous opinions; a sort of jealousy of critical freedom, which, together with the established *nil admirari* of the press, seems to keep them in a constant dread of being thought enthusiastic. They need not be afraid: enthusiasm may belong to such analysis as Schlegel's or Channing's, but has nothing in common with the paragraphs of a newspaper; the inditers of which, in my poor judgment, seldom go beyond the very threshold of criticism, *i. e.* the discovery of faults. I am infinitely amused at the extreme curiosity which appears to me to be the besetting sin of the people here. A gentleman whom you know (as for instance, in my case,) very slightly, will sit down by your table during a morning visit, turn over every article upon it, look at the cards of the various people who have called upon you, ask half-a-dozen questions about each of them, as many about your own private concerns, and all this, as though it were a matter of course that you should answer him, which I feel greatly inclined occasionally not to do.

Saturday, 22d.

Rose at eight. After breakfast, dawdled about till near one o'clock : got into a hackney coach * with D——, and returned all manner of cards.

*　　*　　*　　*　　*

*　　*　　*　　*　　*

Went into a shop to order a pair of shoes. The shopkeepers in this place, with whom I have hitherto had to deal, are either condescendingly familiar, or insolently indifferent in their manner. Your washerwoman sits down before you, while you are *standing* speaking to her ; and a shop-boy bringing things for your inspection, not only sits down, but keeps his hat on in your drawing-room. The worthy man to whom I went for my shoes was so amazingly ungracious, that at first

* The hackney coaches in this country are very different from those perilous receptacles of dust and dirty straw, which disgrace the London stands. They are comfortable within, and clean without; and the horses harnessed to them never exhibit those shocking specimens of cruelty and ill usage which the poor hack horses in London present. Indeed (and it is a circumstance which deserves notice, for it bespeaks general character,) I have not seen, during a two years' residence in this country, a single instance of brutality towards animals, such as one is compelled to witness hourly in the streets of any English town.

I thought I would go out of the shop; but recollecting that I should probably only go farther and fare worse, I gulped, sat down, and was measured. All this is bad: it has its origin in a vulgar misapprehension, which confounds ill breeding with independence, and leads people to fancy that they elevate themselves above their condition by discharging its duties and obligations discourteously.†   *   *   *   *

        *   *   *   *   *

        *   *   *   *   *

Came home: wrote journal, practised, dressed for dinner. At five, went into our neighbour's: Dr. ——, the rector of Grace Church, was the only stranger. I liked him extremely: he sat by me at dinner, and I thought his conversation suf-

----

† There is a striking difference in this respect between the trades-people of New York and those of Boston and Philadelphia; and in my opinion the latter preserve quite self-respect enough to acquit their courtesy and civility from any charge of servility.   The only way in which I can account for the difference, is the greater impulse which trade receives in New York, the proportionate rapidity with which fortunes are made, the ever-shifting materials of which its society is composed, and the facility with which the man who has served you behind his counter, having amassed an independence, assumes a station in the first circle, where his influence becomes commensurate with his wealth. This is not the case either in Boston or Philadelphia; at least, not to the same degree.

ficiently clever, with an abundance of goodness, and liberal benevolent feeling shining through it. We retired to our room, where Mrs. —— made me laugh extremely with sundry passages of her American experiences. I was particularly amused with her account of their stopping, after a long day's journey, at an inn somewhere, when the hostess, who remained in the room the whole time, addressed her as follows: "D' ye play?" pointing to an open piano-forte. Mrs. —— replied that she did so sometimes; whereupon the free and easy landlady ordered candles, and added, "Come, sit down and give us a tune, then;" to which courteous and becoming invitation Mrs. —— replied by taking up her candle, and walking out of the room. The pendant to this is Mr. ——'s story. He sent a die of his crest to a manufacturer to have it put upon his gig harness. The man sent home the harness, when it was finished, but without the die; after sending for which sundry times, Mr. —— called to enquire after it himself, when the reply was : —

"Lord ! why I did'nt know you wanted it."

"I tell you, I wish to have it back."

"Oh, pooh ! you can't want it much, now — do you?"

" I tell you, sir, I desire to have the die back immediately."

" Ah well, come now, what 'll you take for it ? "

" D'ye think I mean to sell my crest ? why you might as well ask me to sell my name."

" Why you see, a good many folks have seen it, and want to have it on their harness, as it's a pretty looking concern enough."

So much for their ideas of a crest. This, though, by the by, happened some years ago.

After the gentlemen joined us, my father made me sing to them, which I did with rather a bad grace, as I don't think any body wished to hear me but himself. *   *   *   *

  *   *   *   *   *

  *   *   *   *   *

Dr. —— is perfectly enchanting. They left us at about eleven. Came to bed.

Sunday, 23d.

Rose at eight. After breakfast, went to church with D——. There is no such thing, I perceive, as a pew-opener ; so, after standing sufficiently long in the middle of the church, we established ourselves very comfortably in a pew, where we remained unmolested. The day was most lovely, and my eyes were constantly attracted to the church windows, through which the magnificent willows of the burial-ground looked like golden-green fountains rising into the sky.   *   *

*   *   *   *   *

*   *   *   *   *

The singing in church was excellent, and Dr. ——'s sermon very good, too: he wants sternness; but that is my particular fancy about a clergyman, and by most people would be accounted no want.   It was not sacrament Sunday; D—— was disappointed, and I mistaken.   Mr. —— walked home with us.   After church, wrote journal.   —— called, and sat with us during dinner, telling us stories of the flogging of slaves, as he himself had witnessed it in the south, that forced the colour into my face, the tears into my eyes, and strained every muscle in my body with positive rage and indignation: he made me perfectly sick with it.   When he was gone, my father went to Colonel ——'s.   I played all through Mr. ——'s edition of Cinderella, and then wrote three long letters, which kept me up till nearly one o'clock.   Oh, bugs, fleas, flies, ants, and musquitoes, great is the misery you inflict upon me!   I sit slapping my own face all day, and lie thumping my pillow all night: 't is a per-

fect nuisance to be devoured of creatures *before*
one's in the ground; it isn't fair. Wrote to Mr.
——, to ask if he would ride with me on Tuesday.
I am dying to be on horseback again.   *

*   *   *   *   *

*   *   *   *   *

Monday, 24th.

Rose at eight: went and took a bath. After
breakfast, went to rehearsal : Venice Preserved,
with Mr. Keppel, who did not appear to me to know
the words even, and seemed perfectly bewildered
at being asked to do the common business of the
piece. " Mercy on me ! what will he do to-
night?" thought I. Came home and got things
ready for the theatre. Received a visit from poor
Mr. ——, who has got the lumbago, as Sir Peter
would say, " on purpose," I believe, to prevent
my riding out to-morrow. Dined at three: after
dinner, played and sang through Cinderella; wrote
journal: at six, went to the theatre. My gown
was horribly ill-plaited, and I looked like a blue-
bag. The house was very full, and they received
Mr. K—— with acclamations and shouts of applause. When I went on, I was all but tumbling
down at the sight of my Jaffier, who looked like

the apothecary in Romeo and Juliet, with the
addition of some devilish red slashes along his
thighs and arms. The first scene passed well and
so : but, oh, the next, and the next, and the next
to that. Whenever he was not glued to my side
(and that was seldom), he stood three yards behind me ; he did nothing but seize my hand, and
grapple to it so hard, that unless I had knocked
him down (which I felt much inclined to try), I could
not disengage myself. In the senate scene, when
I was entreating for mercy, and *struggling*, as
Otway has it, for my life, he was prancing round
the stage in every direction, flourishing his dagger
in the air : I wish to Heaven I had got up and
run away; it would but have been natural, and
have served him extremely right. In the parting
scene, — oh what a scene it was ! — instead of
going away from me when he said " farewell for
ever," he stuck to my skirts, though in the same
breath that I adjured him, in the words of my
part, not to leave me, I added, aside, " Get away
from me, oh *do !*" When I exclaimed, " Not
one kiss at parting," he kept embracing and kiss-
ing me like mad ; and when I ought to have been
pursuing him, and calling after him, " Leave thy
dagger with me," he hung himself up against the
wing, and remained dangling there for five

minutes. I was half crazy! and the good people sat and swallowed it all: they deserved it, by my troth, they did. I prompted him constantly, and once, after struggling in vain to free myself from him, was obliged, in the middle of my part, to exclaim, "You hurt me dreadfully, Mr. Keppel!" He clung to me, cramped me, crumpled me, — dreadful! I never experienced any thing like this before, and made up my mind that I never would again. I played of course like a wretch, finished my part as well as I could, and, as soon as the play was over, went to my father and Mr. Simpson, and declared to them both my determination not to go upon the stage again, with that gentleman for a hero. Three trials are as many as, in reason, any body can demand, and come what come may, *I* will not be subjected to this sort of experiment again. At the end of the play, the clever New Yorkians actually called for Mr. Keppel! and this most worthless clapping of hands, most worthlessly bestowed upon such a worthless object, is what, by the nature of my craft, I am bound to care for; I spit at it from the bottom of my soul! Talking of applause, the man who acted Bedamar to-night thought fit to be two hours dragging me off the stage; in consequence of which I had to scream, " Jaffier,

Jaffier," till I thought I should have broken a blood-vessel. On my remonstrating with him upon this, he said, " Well, you are rewarded, listen :" the people were clapping and shouting vehemently: this is the whole history of acting and actors. We came home tired, and thoroughly disgusted, and found no supper. The cooks, who do not live in the house, but come and do their work, and depart home whenever it suits their convenience, had not thought proper to stay to prepare any supper for us : so we had to wait for the readiest things that could be procured out of doors for us — this was pleasant * — very ! At

* The universal hour of dining, in New York, when first we arrived, was three o'clock; after which hour the cooks took their departure, and nothing was to be obtained fit to eat, either for love or money : this intolerable nuisance is gradually passing away; but even now, though we can get our dinner served at six o'clock, it is always dressed at three; its excellence may be imagined from that. To say the truth, I think the system upon which all houses of public entertainment are conducted in this country is a sample of the patience and long-suffering with which dirt, discomfort, and exorbitant charges may be borne by a whole community, without resistance, or even remonstrance. The best exceptions I could name to these various inconveniences are, first, Mr. Cozzen's establishment at West Point; next, the Tremont at Boston, and, lastly, the Mansion House at Philadelphia. In each of these, wayfarers may obtain some portion of decent comfort: but they have their drawbacks;

last appeared a cold boiled fowl, and some monstrous oysters, that looked for all the world like an antediluvian race of oysters, " for in those days there were giants." Six mouthfuls each : they were well-flavoured ; but their size displeased my eye, and I swallowed but one, and came to bed.

Friday, 28th.

A letter from England, the first from dear ——.
D—— brought it me while I was dressing, and oh, how welcome, how welcome it was !   *

* * * * *

After breakfast went to rehearsal : Much Ado about Nothing. Came home, wrote journal, put out things for the theatre, dined at three. After dinner, —— called.

---

in the first, there are no private sitting rooms; and in the last, the number of servants is inadequate to the work. The Tremont is by far the best establishment of the sort existing at present. Mr. A——, the millionaire of New York, is about to remedy this deficiency, by the erection of a magnificent hotel in Broadway. One thing, however, is certain ; neither he nor any one else will ever succeed in having a decent house, if the servants are not a little superior to the Irish savages who officiate in that capacity in most houses, public and private, in the northern states of America.

* * * * *

* * * * *

Mr. —— called, and sat with us till six o'clock.

 * * * * *

 * * * * *

I constantly sit thunderstruck at the amazing number of unceremonious questions which people here think fit to ask one, and, moreover, expect one to answer. Went to the theatre; the house was not good. The Italians were expected to sing for the first time; they did not, however, but in the mean time thinned our house.

I would give the world to see Mr. —— directing the public taste, by an oeiliad, and leading the public approbation, by a gracious tapping of his supreme hand upon his ineffable snuff-box; he reminds me of high life below stairs. The play went off very well; I played well, and my dresses looked beautiful; my father acted to perfection. I never saw any thing so gallant, gay, so like a gentleman, so full of brilliant, buoyant, refined spirit; he looked admirably, too. Mr. —— was behind the scenes: speaking to me of my father's appearance in Pierre, he said he reminded him of Lord ——. I could not forbear asking him how long he had been away from England: he replied, four years. Truly, four years will furnish him matter of astonishment when he returns. Swallow Street is grown into a line of palaces; the Strand is a broad magnificent avenue, where all the wealth of the world seems gathered together; and Lord ——, the " observed of all observers," is become a red-faced, fat old man. " Och, Time! can't ye be aisy now!"

Sunday, 30th.

Rose late, did not go to church; sat writing letters all the morning. Mr. —— and Mr. —— called. What a character that Mr. —— is. Colonel —— called, and wanted to take my father out; but we were all inditing epistles to go to-morrow by the dear old Pacific. At three o'clock, went to church with Mrs. —— and Mr. ——. I like Dr. —— most extremely. His mild, benevolent, Christian view of the duties and blessings of life is very delightful; and the sound practical doctrine he preaches " good for edification."   *   *   *   *

     *   *   *   *   *

It poured with rain, but they sent a coach for us from the inn; came home, dressed for dinner. D—— and I dined *tête-à-tête*. After dinner, sat writing letters for Mr. ——'s bag till ten o'clock:

came to my own room, undressed, and began a volume to dear ——.　*　　　*　　　*

　*　　　*　　　*　　　*　　　*

　*　　　*　　　*　　　*　　　*

I did not get to bed till three o'clock : in spite of all which I am as fat as an overstuffed pincushion.

　*　　　*　　　*　　　*　　　*

　*　　　*　　　*　　　*　　　*

Select specimens of American pronunciation : —

vaggaries,	vagaries.
ad infínnitum,	ad infinitem.
vitúpperate,	vituperate.

Monday, October 1st.

While I was out, Captain —— called for our letters.　Saw Mr. ——, and bade him good-by : they are going away to-day to Havre, to Europe ; I wish I was a nail in one of their trunks.　After breakfast, went to rehearse King John : what a lovely mess they will make of it, to be sure. When my sorrows were ended, my father brought me home : found a most lovely nosegay from Mr. —— awaiting me.　Bless it ! how sweet it smelt, and how pretty it looked.　Spent an hour delightfully in putting it into water.　Got things ready for to-night, practised till dinner, and wrote

journal.   My father received a letter to-day, informing him that a cabal was forming by the
friends of Miss Vincent and Miss Clifton (native
talent!) to hiss us off the New York stage, if possible; if not, to send people in every night to
create a disturbance during our best scenes: the
letter is anonymous, and therefore little deserving
of attention.   After dinner, practised till time to
go to the theatre.   The house was very full; but
what a cast! what a play! what botchers! what
butchers!   In his very first scene, the most christian king stuck fast; and there he stood, shifting
his truncheon from hand to hand, rolling his eyes,
gasping for breath, and struggling for words,
like a man in the night-mare.   I thought of
Hamlet — "Leave thy damnable faces"—and was
obliged to turn away.   In the scene before An-
giers, when the French and English heralds summon the citizens to the walls, the Frenchman
applied his instrument to his mouth, uplifted his
chest, distended his cheeks, and appeared to blow
furiously; not a sound! he dropped his arm, and
looked off the stage in discomfiture and indignation, when the perverse trumpet set up a blast
fit to waken the dead, — the audience roared: it
reminded me of the harp in the old ballad, that

" began to play alone." Chatillon, on his return from England, begged to assure us that with King John was come the mother queen, an *Anty* stirring him to blood and war. When Cardinal Pandulph came on, the people set up a shout, as usual: he was dreadfully terrified, poor thing; and all the time he spoke kept giving little nervous twitches to his sacred petticoat, in a fashion that was enough to make one die of laughter. He was as obstinate, too, in his bewilderment as a stuttering man in his incoherency; for once, when he stuck fast, having twitched his skirts, and thumped his breast in vain for some time, I thought it best, having to speak next, to go on; when, lo and behold! in the middle of my speech, the " scarlet sin " recovers his memory, and shouts forth the end of his own, to the utter confusion of my august self and the audience. I thought they never would have got through my last scene: king gazed at cardinal, and cardinal gazed at king; king nodded and winked at the prompter, spread out his hands, and remained with his mouth open: cardinal nodded and winked at the prompter, crossed his hands on his breast, and remained with his mouth open; neither of them uttering a syllable! What a scene! O, what a glorious scene! Came home as soon as my part was over. Supped, and sat up for my father. Heard his account of the end, and came to bed.*

Wednesday, 3d.

Rose late. After breakfast, went to rehearsal: what a mess I do make of Bizarre! Ellen Tree and Mrs. Chatterly were angels to what I shall be, yet I remember thinking them both bad enough. After all, if people generally did but know the difficulty of doing well, they would be less damnatory upon those who do ill. It is not easy to act well. After rehearsal, went to Stewart's with D——. As we were proceeding up Broadway

---

* It is fortunate for the managers of the Park Theatre, and very unfortunate for the citizens of New York, that the audiences who frequent that place of entertainment are chiefly composed of the strangers who are constantly passing in vast numbers through this city. It is not worth the while of the management to pay a good company, when an indifferent one answers their purpose quite as well: the system upon which theatrical speculations are conducted in this country is, having one or two "stars" for the principal characters, and nine or ten sticks for all the rest. The consequence is, that a play is never decently acted, and at such times as stars are scarce, the houses are very deservedly empty. The terrestrial audiences suffer much by this mode of getting up plays; but the celestial performers, the stars propped upon sticks, infinitely more.

to Bonfanti's*, I saw a man in the strangest attitude imaginable, absolutely setting at us : presently he pounced, and who should it be but ——. He came into Bonfanti's with us, and afterwards insisted on escorting us to our various destinations ; not, however, without manifold and deep lamentations on his slovenly appearance and dirty gloves. The latter, however, he managed to exchange *chemin faisant* for a pair of new ones, which he extracted from his pocket and drew on, without letting go our arms, which he squeezed most unmercifully during the operation. We went through a part of the town which I had never seen before. The shops have all a strange fair-like appearance, and exhibit a spectacle of heterogeneous disorder, which greatly amazes the eye of a Londoner. The comparative infancy in which most of the adornments of life are yet in this country, renders it impossible for the number of distinct trades to exist, that do among us, where the population is so much denser, and where the luxurious indulgences of the few find ample occupation for the penurious industry of the many. But here, one man drives several trades; and in every shop you meet with a strange incongruous mixture of articles

* Stewart — Bonfanti. The name of shopkeepers in Broadway : the former's is the best shop in New York.

for sale, which would be found nowhere in England, but in the veriest village huckster's. Comparatively few of the objects for sale can be exposed in the windows, which are unlike our shop windows, narrow and ill adapted for the display of goods : but piles of them lie outside the doors, choking up the pathway, and coloured cloths, flannels, shawls, &c., are suspended about in long draperies, whose vivid colours flying over the face of the houses give them an untidy, but at the same time a gay, flaunting appearance. We went into a shop to buy some stockings, and missing our *preux chevalier*, I turned round to look for him ; when I perceived him beautifying most busily before a glass in a further corner of the shop. He had seized on a sort of house brush, and began brooming his hat : the next operation was to produce a small pocket comb and arrange his disordered locks ; lastly, he transferred the services of the brush of all work from his head to his feet, and having dusted his boots, drawn himself up in his surtout, buttoned its two lower buttons, and given a reforming grasp to his neckcloth, he approached us, evidently much advanced in his own good graces. We went to the furrier's, and brought away my dark boa. Came home, put out things for packing up, and remained so engaged till time to dress for

143

dinner. Mr. and Mrs. —— and Mr. —— dined
with us.

* * * * *

* * * * *

Mr. —— is an Englishman of the high breed,
and sufficiently pleasant. After dinner we had to
withdraw into our bed-room, for the house is so
full that they can't cram any thing more into an
inch of it.

Joined the gentlemen at tea. Mr. —— had
gone to the theatre: Mr. —— and I had some
music. He plays delightfully, and knows every
note of music that ever was written; but he had the
barbarity to make me sing a song of his own com-
posing to him, which is a cruel thing in a man to
do. He went away at about eleven, and we then
came to bed. My father went to see Miss Clifton,
at the Bowery theatre.

Thursday, 4th.

Rose late. After breakfast, went to rehearsal: my
Bizarre is getting a little more into shape. After
rehearsal, came home. Mr. —— and Mr. ——
called, and sat some time with me. The former
is tolerably pleasant, but a little too fond of telling
good stories that he has told before. Put out things

for the theatre: dined at three.   Colonel ——
called. Wrote journal : while doing so, was called
out to look at my gown, which the worthy milliner
had sent home.

> I am, I am an angel! Witness it, heaven !
> Witness it earth, and every being witness it!
> The gown was spoil'd !   Yet by immortal patience
> I did not even fly into a passion.

She took it back to alter it.   Presently arrived my
wreath, and that had also to be taken back ; for
't was nothing like what I had ordered.   Now all
this does not provoke me ; but the thing that does,
is the dreadful want of manners of the trades-people
here.   They bolt into your room without knocking,
nod to you, sit down, and without the preface of
either Sir, Ma'am, or Miss, start off into " Well
now, I 'm come to speak about so and so." At six,
went to the theatre; play, the Hunchback : the
house was crammed from floor to ceiling.   I had
an intense headache, but played tolerably well.   I
wore my red satin, and looked like a bonfire. Came
home and found Smith's Virginia, and two volumes
of Graham's America, which I want to read. They
charge twelve dollars for these : every thing is
horribly dear here.   Came to bed with my head
splitting.

Friday, 5th.

Played Bizarre for the first time. Acted so-so, looked very pretty, the house was very fine, and my father incomparable : they called for him after the play. Colonel —— and Mr. —— called in while we were at supper.

Saturday, 6th.

Rose late: when I came in to breakfast, found Colonel —— sitting in the parlour. He remained for a long time, and we had sundry discussions on topics manifold. It seems that the blessed people here were shocked at my having to hear the coarseness of Farquhar's Inconstant — humbug ! † *

 *   *   *   *   *

* Were the morality that I constantly hear uttered a little more consistent, not only with right reason, but with itself, I think it might be more deserving of attention and respect. But the mock delicacy, which exists to so great a degree with regard to theatrical exhibitions, can command neither the one nor the other. To those who forbid all dramatic representations, as exhibitions of an unhealthy tendency upon our intellectual and moral nature, I have no objections, at present, to make. Unqualified condemnation, particularly when adopted on such grounds, may be a sincere, a respectable, perhaps a right, opinion. I have but one reply to offer to it : the human mind requires recreation ; is not a theatre, (always supposing it to be, not what theatres too

At twelve, went out shopping, and paying bills; called upon Mrs. ———, and sat some time with

---

often are, but what they ought to be,) is not a theatre a better, a higher, a more noble, and useful place of recreation than a billiard-room, or the bar of a tavern ? Perhaps in the course of the moral and intellectual improvement of mankind, *all* these will give way to yet purer and more refined sources of recreation; but in the mean time, I confess, with its manifold abuses, a play-house appears to me worthy of toleration, if not of approbation, as holding forth (when directed as it should be) a highly intellectual, rational, and refined amusement.

However, as I before said, my quarrel is not with those who condemn indiscriminately all theatrical exhibitions; they may be right: at all events, so sweeping a sentence betrays no inconsistency. But what are we to say to individuals, or audiences, who turn with affected disgust from the sallies of Bizarre and Beatrice, and who applaud and laugh, and are delighted at the gross immorality of such plays as the Wonder, and Rule a Wife and have a Wife; the latter particularly, in which the immorality and indecency are not those of expression only, but of conception, and mingle in the whole construction of the piece, in which not one character appears whose motives of action are not most unworthy, and whose language is not as full of coarseness, as devoid of every generous, elevated, or refined sentiment. (The tirades of Leon are no exception; for in the mouth of a man who marries such a woman as Marguerita, by such means, and for such an end, they are mere mockeries.) I confess that my surprise was excited when I was told that an American audience would not endure that portion of Beatrice's wit, which the London censors have spared, and that Othello was all but a proscribed play; but it was infinitely

her and Mrs. ———; left a card at Mrs. ———'s,
and came home, prepared things for our journey,

---

more so, when I found that the same audience tolerated, or
rather encouraged with their presence and applause, the
coarse production of Mrs. Centlivre and Beaumont and
Fletcher. With regard to the Inconstant, it is by far the
most moral of Farquhar's plays; that, perhaps, is little
praisé, for the Recruiting Officer, and the Beau's Stratagem,
are decidedly the reverse. But in spite of the licentiousness
of the writing, in many parts, the construction, the motive,
the action of the play is not licentious; the characters are
far from being utterly debased in their conception, or de-
praved in the sentiments they utter (excepting, of course,
the companions of poor Mirable's last revel); the women,
those surest criterions, by whose principles and conduct
may be formed the truest opinion of the purity of the social
atmosphere, the women, though free in their manners and
language, (it was the fashion of their times, and of the times
before them, when words did not pass for deeds, either good
or bad,) are essentially honest women; and Bizarre, coarse
as her expressions may appear, has yet more *real* delicacy
than poor Oriana, whose womanly love causes her too far to
forget her womanly pride. Of the catastrophe of this play,
and its frightfully pointed moral, little need be said to prove
that its effect is likely to be far more wholesome, because
far more homely, than that of most theatrical inventions; invention, indeed, it is not, and its greatest interest, as perhaps
its chief utility, is drawn from the circumstance of its being
a faithful representation of a situation of unequalled horror,
in which the author himself was placed, and from which he
was rescued precisely as he extricates his hero. Of the
truth and satirical power of the dialogue, none who understand it can dispute, and if, instead of attaching themselves

and dressed for dinner. On our way to Mr.
——'s, my father told me he had been seeing Miss

---

to the farcical romping of Bizarre and her ungallant lover,
the modest critics of this play had devoted some attention
to the dialogues between young and old Mirable, their nice
sense of decency would have been less shocked, and they
might have found themselves repaid by some of the most
pointed, witty, and pithy writing in the English dramatic
literature. I am much obliged to such of my friends as
lamented that I had to personate Farquhar's impertinent
heroine; for my own good part, I would as lief be such an
one, as either Jane Shore, Mrs. Haller, Lady Macbeth, or
the wild woman Bianca. I know that great crimes have a
species of evil grandeur in them; they spring only from a
powerful soil, they are in their very magnitude respectable.
I know that mighty passions have in their very excess a
frightful majesty, that asserts the vigour of the natures from
which they rise; and there is as little similarity between
them, and the base, degraded, selfish, cowardly tribe of petty
larceny vices with which human societies abound, as there is
between the caterpillar blight, that crawls over a fertile dis-
trict, gnawing it away inch-meal, and the thunderbolt that
scathes, or the earthquake that swallows the same region, in
its awful mission of destruction. But I maintain that freedom of expression and manner is by no means an indication
of laxity of morals, and again repeat that Bizarre is free in
her words, but not in her principles. The authoress of the
most graceful and true analysis of Shakspeare's female characters has offered a better vindication of their manners
than I could write; I can only say, I pity sincerely all those
who, passing over the exquisite purity, delicacy, and loveliness of their conception, dwell only upon modes of expression which belong to the times in which their great creator

Clifton, the girl they want him to teach to act; (to *teach* to act, quotha ! ! !) he says, she is very pretty,

---

lived. With respect to the manner in which audiences are affected by what they hear on the stage, I cannot but think that gentlemen who wish their wives and daughters to hear no language of an exceptionable nature, had better make themselves acquainted with what they take them to see, or at all events, avoid, when in the theatre, attracting their attention to expressions which their disapprobation serves only to bring into notice, and which had much better escape unheard, or at least unheeded. Voluminous as this note has become, I cannot but add one word with respect to the members of the profession to which I have belonged. Many actresses that I have known, in the performance of unvirtuous or unlovely characters, (I cannot, however, help remembering that they were also secondary parts,) have thought fit to impress the audience with the wide difference between their assumed and real disposition, by acting as ill, and looking as cross as they possibly could, which could not but be a great satisfaction to any moral audience. I have seen this done by that fine part in Milman's Fazio, Aldabella, repeatedly, and not unfrequently by the Queen in Hamlet, Margarita in Rule a Wife and have a Wife, (I scarcely wonder at that, though,) and even by poor Shakspeare's Lady Falconbridge. I think this is a mistake: the audience, I believe, never forget that the actress is not indeed the wicked woman she seems. In one instance that might have been the case, perhaps. I speak of a great artist, whose efforts I never witnessed, but whose private excellence I have a near right to rejoice in, and who was as true in her performance of the wretch Millwood, as in her personifications of Shakspeare's grandest creations.

indeed, with fine eyes, a fair, delicate skin, and a
handsome mouth; moreover, a tall woman, and
yet from the front of the house her effect is nought.
What a pity, and a provoking ! A pleasant dinner,
very.   Mr. —— the poet, one Dr. ——, Colonel
——, and Mr. —— : the only woman was a Miss
——   *   *   *   *

   *   *   *   *   *

   *   *   *   *   *

——'s face reminded me of young —— : the countenance was not quite so good, but there was the
same radiant look about the eyes and forehead·
His expression was strongly sarcastic; I liked him
very much, notwithstanding.   When we left the
men, we had the pleasure of the children's society,
and that of an unhappy kitten, whom a little pitiless
urchin of three years old was carrying crumpled
under her arm like a pincushion.   The people
here make me mad by abusing Lawrence's drawing
of me. If ever there was a refined and intellectual
work, where the might of genius triumphing over
every material impediment has enshrined and
embodied spirit itself, it is that.   Talking of Lawrence, (poor Lawrence !) Mrs. —— said, " Ah,
yes ! your picture by—a—Sir—something—Lawrence !"   Oh, fame ! oh, fame ! Oh, vanity and
vexation of spirit ! does your eternity and your

infinitude amount to this? There are lands where Shakspeare's name was never heard, where Raphael and Handel are unknown; to be sure, for the matter of that, there are regions (and those wide ones too) where Jesus Christ is unknown. At nine o'clock, went to the Richmond Hill theatre, to see the opening of the Italian company. The house itself is a pretty little box enough, but as bad as a box to sing in. We went to Mr. ——'s box, where he was kind enough to give us seats. The first act was over, but we had all the benefit of the second. I had much ado not to laugh ; and when Mr. ——, that everlasting gigler, came and sat down beside me, I gave myself up for lost. However, I did behave in spite of two blue bottles of women, who by way of the sisters buzzed about the stage, singing enough to set one's teeth on edge. Then came a very tall Dandini ; by the by, that man had a good bass voice, but Mr. —— said it was the finest he had heard since *Zucchelli.* O tempora ! O mores ! Zucchelli, that prince of delicious baritones ! However, as I said, the man has a good bass voice ; there was also a sufficiently good Pompolino. Montresor banged himself about, broke his time, and made some execrable flourishes in the Prince, whereat the enlightened New Yorkians applauded mightily.

But the Prima Donna ! but the Cenerentola ! Cospetto di Venere, what a figure, and what a face! Indeed she was the very thing for a lower housemaid, and I think the Prince was highly to blame for removing her from the station nature had evidently intended her for. She was old and ugly, and worse than ugly, unpardonably common-looking, with a cast in her eye, and a foot that, as Mr. —— observed, it would require a *pretty considerable* large glass slipper to fit. Then she sang — discords and dismay, how she did sing ! I could not forbear stealing a glance at ——: he applauded the sestett vehemently; but when it came to that most touching " *nacqui al' affanno* " he wisely interposed his handkerchief between the stage and his gracious countenance. I thought of poor dear —— and her sweet voice, and her refined taste, and shuddered to hear this favourite of hers bedevilled by such a Squalini. Now is it possible that people can be such fools as to fancy this good in spite of their senses, or such earless asses (that's a bull I suppose), as to suffer themselves to be persuaded that it is ? Though why do I ask it? Oh yes, " very easily possible." Do not half the people in London spend money and time without end, enduring nightly penances — listening to what hey can't understand, and couldn't appreciate if they did? I suppose if I shall allow a hundred out of the whole King's Theatre audience to know any thing whatever about music, I am wide in my grant of comprehension. There was that virtuous youth, Mr. ——, who evidently ranks as one of the cognoscenti here, who exclaimed triumphantly at the end of one of the perpetrations, " Well, after all, there 's nothing like Rossini." Handel, Haydn, Mosart, Beethoven, and Weber, are *not*, that is certain.* I wish I could have seen Mr. ——

---

* The Russians and Danes are rich in the possession of an original and most touching national music; Scotland, Ireland, and Wales, are alike favoured with the most exquisite native melodies, probably, in the world. France, though more barren in the wealth of sweet sounds, has a few fine old airs, that redeem her from the charge of utter sterility. Austria, Bohemia, and Switzerland, each claim a thousand beautiful and characteristic mountain songs; Italy is the very palace of music, Germany its temple; Spain resounds with wild and martial strains, and the thick groves of Portugal with native music, of a softer and sadder kind. All the nations of Europe, I presume all those of all the world, possess some kind of national music, and are blessed by Heaven with some measure of perception as to the loveliness of harmonious sounds. England alone, England and her descendant America, seems to have been denied a sense, to want a capacity, to have been stinted of a faculty, to the possession of which she vainly aspires. The rich spirit of Italian music, the solemn soul of German melody, the wild free Euterpe of the Cantons, have in vain been summoned by turns to teach her how to listen; 't is all in vain — she

during that finale.   Coming out, were joined by
Mr. ——— : brought him home in the carriage
with us.   Gave him " Ye mariners of Spain," and
some cold tongue, to take the taste of the Cenerentola out of his mouth.   He stayed some time.
I like him enough : he is evidently a clever man,
though he does murder the King's English.   (By
the by, does *English*, the tongue, belong, in America, to the King or the President — I wonder?
I should rather think, from my limited observations, that it was the individual property of every
freeborn citizen of the United States.)   Now, what
on earth can I say to the worthy citizens, if they
ask me what I thought of the Italian opera !   That
it was very amusing — yes, that will do nicely ;
that will be true, and not too direct a condemnation
of their good taste.

---

does listen painfully ; she has learnt by dint of time, and
much endurance, the technicalities of musical science ; she
pays regally her instructors in the divine pleasure, but all in
vain : the spirit of melody is not in her ; and in spite of hosts
of foreign musicians, in spite of the King's Theatre, in spite
of Pasta, in spite of music-masters paid like ministers of
state, in spite of singing and playing young ladies, and criti-
cising young gentlemen, England, to the last day of her
life, will be a dunce in music, for she hath it not in her ;
neither, if I am not much mistaken, hath her daughter.

Sunday, 7th.

Rose late. Young —— breakfasted with us. How unfortunately plain he is! His voice is marvellously like his father's, and it pleased me to hear him speak therefore. He was talking to my father about the various southern and western theatres, and bidding us expect to meet strange coadjutors in those lost lands beyond the world. On one occasion he said, when he was acting Richard the Third, some of the underlings kept their hats on while he was on the stage, whereat —— remonstrated, requesting them in a whisper to uncover, as they were in the presence of a king; to which admonition he received the following characteristic reply: " Fiddlestick! I guess we know nothing about kings in this country." Colonel —— called too; but D—— and I went off to church, and left my father to entertain them. Met Mr. —— and Mr. ——, who were coming to fetch us: went to Mr. ——'s pew. The music was very delightful; but decidedly I do not like music in church. The less my senses are appealed to in the house of prayer the better for me and my devotions. Although I have experienced excitement of a stern and martial, and sometimes of a solemn, nature, from music, yet these melt away, and its abiding influence with me is of a much softer kind : therefore, in church, I had rather dispense with it, particularly when they sing psalms, as they did to-day, to the tune of " Come dwell with me, and be my love." I did not like the sermon much ; there was effect in it, painting, which I dislike. Staid the sacrament, the first I have taken in this strange land. Mr. —— walked home with us : when he was gone, Mr. —— and Mr. —— called. When they had all taken their departure, settled accounts, wrote journal, wrote to my mother, came and put away sundry things, and dressed for dinner. My father dined with Mr. —— : D—— and I dined *tête-à-tête.* Colonel —— came twice through the pouring rain to look after our baggage for to-morrow ; such charity is unexampled.

Monday, 8*th.*

Rose (oh, horror !) at a quarter to five. Night was still brooding over the earth. Long before I was dressed the first voice I heard was that of Colonel ——, come to look after our luggage, and see us off. To lend my friend a thousand pounds (if I had it) I could ; to lend him my horse, per-

haps I might; but to get up in the middle of the
night, and come dawdling in the grey cold hour
of the morning upon damp quays, and among
dusty packages, except for my own flesh and blood,
I could not. Yet this worthy man did it for us;
whence I pronounce that he must be half a Quaker
himself, for no common episcopal benevolence
could stretch this pitch. Dressed, and gathered
together my things, and at six o'clock, just as the
night was folding its soft black wings, and rising
slowly from the earth, we took our departure from
that mansion of little ease, the American, and our
fellow-lodgers the ants, and proceeded to the Philadelphia steam-boat, which started from the bottom
of Barclay Street. We were recommended to this
American hotel as the best and most comfortable
in New York; and truly the charges were as high
as one could have paid at the Clarendon, in the
land of comfort and taxation. The wine was
exorbitantly dear; champagne and claret about
eleven shillings sterling a bottle; sherry, port, and
madeira, from nine to thirteen. The rooms were
a mixture of French finery, and Irish disorder
and dirt; the living was by no means good; the
whole house being conducted on a close scraping
system of inferior accommodations and extrava-
gant charges. On a sudden influx of visiters,

sitting-rooms were converted into bed-rooms, containing four and five beds. The number of servants was totally inadequate to the work; and the articles of common use, such as knives and spoons, were so scantily provided, that when the public table was very full one day, the knives and forks for our dinner were obliged to be washed from theirs; and the luxury of a carving knife was not to be procured at all on that occasion: it is true that they had sometimes as many as two hundred and fifty guests at the ordinary. The servants, who, as I said before, were just a quarter as many as the house required, had no bed-rooms allotted to them, but slept *about* any where, in the public rooms, or on sofas in drawing-rooms, let to private families. In short, nothing can exceed the want of order, propriety, and comfort in this establishment, except the enormity of the tribute it levies upon pilgrims and wayfarers through the land.* And so, as I said, we departed therefrom nothing loath.

The morning was dull, dreary, and damp, which

* It is but justice to state, that this house has passed into other hands, and is much improved in every respect. Strangers, particularly Englishmen, will find a great convenience in the five o'clock ordinary, now established there which is, I am told, excellently conducted and appointed.

I regretted very much. The steam-boat was very large and commodious, as all these conveyances are. I enquired of one of the passengers what the power of the engine was : he replied that he did not exactly know, but that he thought it was about forty-horse power; and that, when going at speed, the engine struck thirty times in a minute : this appeared to me a great number in so short a time; but the weather shortly became wet and drizzly, and I did not remain on deck to observe. My early rising had made me very sleepy, so I came down to the third deck to sleep. These steamboats have three stories; the upper one is, as it were, a roofing or terrace on the leads of the second, a very desirable station when the weather is neither too foul nor too fair; a burning sun being, I should think, as little desirable there as a shower of rain. The second floor or deck has the advantage of the ceiling above, and yet, the sides being completely open, it is airy, and allows free sight of the shores on either hand. Chairs, stools, and benches, are the furniture of these two decks. The one below, or third floor, downwards, in fact, the *ground floor*, being the one near the water, is a spacious room completely roofed and walled in, where the passengers take their meals, and resort if the weather is unfavourable.

At the end of this room is a smaller cabin for the use of the ladies, with beds and a sofa, and all the conveniences necessary, if they should like to be sick; whither I came and slept till breakfast time. Vigne's account of the pushing, thrusting, rushing, and devouring on board a western steamboat at meal times had prepared me for rather an awful spectacle; but this, I find, is by no means the case in these more civilised parts, and every thing was conducted with perfect order, propriety, and civility. The breakfast was good, and served and eaten with decency enough. Came up on the upper deck, and walked about with my father. The width of the river struck me as remarkable; but the shores were flat, and for the most part uninteresting, except for the rich and various tints which the thickets of wood presented, and which are as superior in brilliancy and intenseness to our autumnal colouring as their gorgeous skies are to ours. Opposite the town of Amboy, the Raritan opens into a magnificent lake-like expanse round the extreme point of Staten Island.* As

* The whole of this passage is in fact a succession of small bays, forming a continuation to the grand bay of New York, and dividing Staten Island from the mainland of New Jersey; the Raritan river does not properly begin till Amboy, where it empties itself into a bay of its own name.

the shores on either side, however, were not very interesting, I finished reading Combe's book. There is much sound philosophy in it; but I do not think it altogether establishes the main point that he wishes to make good — the truth of phrenology, and the necessity of its being adopted as the only science of the human mind. His general assertions admit of strong individual exceptions, which, I think, go far towards invalidating the generality. However, 't is not a full developement of his own system, but, as it were, only an introduction to it; and his own admissions of the obscurity and uncertainty in which that system is still involved necessarily enforces a suspension of judgment, until its practical results have become more manifest, and in some measure borne witness to the truth of his theory.—At about half-past ten we reached the place where we leave the river, to proceed across a part of the State of New Jersey to the Delaware. The landing was beyond measure wretched: the shore shelved down to the water's edge; and its marshy, clayey, sticky soil, rendered doubly soft and squashy by the damp weather, was strewn over with broken potsherds, stones, and bricks, by way of pathway; these, however, presently failed, and some slippery planks half immersed in mud were the only roads to the

coaches that stood ready to receive the passengers
of the steam-boat. Oh, these coaches! English
eye hath not seen, English ear hath not heard, nor
hath it entered into the heart of Englishmen to
conceive the surpassing clumsiness and wretchedness of these leathern inconveniences. They are
shaped something like boats, the sides being merely
leathern pieces, removable at pleasure, but which,
in bad weather, are buttoned down to protect the
inmates from the wet. There are three seats in
this machine; the middle one, having a movable
leathern strap, by way of adossier, runs between
the carriage doors, and lifts away to permit the
egress and ingress of the occupants of the other
seats. Into the one facing the horses D—— and
I put ourselves; presently two young ladies occupied the opposite one; a third lady, and a gentleman of the same party, sat in the middle seat, into
which my father's huge bulk was also squeezed;
finally, another man belonging to the same party
ensconced himself between the two young ladies.
Thus the two seats were filled, each with three
persons, and there should by rights have been a
third on ours; for this nefarious black hole on
wheels is intended to carry nine. However, we
profited little by the space, for, letting alone that
there is not really and truly room for more than

two human beings of common growth and proportions on each of these seats, the third place
was amply filled up with baskets and packages of
ours, and huge *undoubleableup* coats and cloaks of
my father's. For the first few minutes I thought
I must have fainted from the intolerable sensation
of smothering which I experienced. However,
the leathers having been removed, and a little
more air obtained, I took heart of grace, and re-
signed myself to my fate. Away wallopped the
four horses, trotting with their front, and galloping
with their hind legs; and away went we after them,
bumping, thumping, jumping, jolting, shaking,
tossing, and tumbling, over the wickedest road, I
do think the cruellest, hard-heartedest road that
ever wheel rumbled upon. Thorough bog and
marsh, and ruts wider and deeper than any christian ruts I ever saw, with the roots of trees pro-
truding across our path; their boughs every now
and then giving us an affectionate scratch through
the windows; and, more than once, a half-demo-
lished trunk or stump lying in the middle of the
road lifting us up, and letting us down again, with
most awful variations of our poor coach body from
its natural position. Bones of me! what a road!*

* I had always heard that the face of nature was gigantic
in America; and truly we found the wrinkles such for so
young a country. The ruts were absolute abysses.

Even my father's solid proportions could not keep
their level, but were jerked up to the roof and
down again every three minutes.   Our companions
seemed nothing dismayed by these wondrous performances of a coach and four, but laughed and
talked incessantly, the young ladies, at the very top
of their voices, and with the national nasal twang.*
The conversation was much of the *genteel* shop-
keeper kind; the wit of the ladies, and the gallantry
of the gentlemen, savouring strongly of tapes and
yard measures, and the shrieks of laughter of the
whole set enough to drive one into a frenzy.
The ladies were all pretty; two of them particularly so, with delicate fair complexions, and beau-

---

* The southern, western, and eastern states of North
America have each their strong peculiarities of enunciation,
which render them easy of recognition.   The Virginian and
New England accents appear to me the most striking;
Pennsylvania and New York have much less brogue; but
through all their various tones and pronunciations a very
strong nasal inflection preserves their universal brotherhood.
They all speak through their noses, and at the top of their
voices.   Of dialects, properly so called, there are none;
though a few expressions, peculiar to particular states,
which generally serve to identify their citizens; but these
are not numerous, and a jargon approaching in obscurity
that of many of our counties is not to be met with.   The
language used in society generally is unrefined, inelegant,
and often ungrammatically vulgar; but it is more vulgar than
unintelligible by far.

tiful grey eyes: how I wish they could have held
their tongues for two minutes.   We had not long
been in the coach before one of them complained
of being dreadfully sick.*   This, in such a space,
and with seven near neighbours !   Fortunately she
was near the window; and during our whole fourteen miles of purgatory she alternately leaned
from it overcome with sickness, then reclined lan-
guishingly in the arms of her next neighbour, and
then, starting up with amazing vivacity, joined her
voice to the treble duet of her two pretty companions, with a superiority of shrillness, that might
have been the pride and envy of Billingsgate.
'T was enough to bother a rookery !   The country
through which we passed was woodland, flat, and
without variety, save what it derived from the
wondrous richness and brilliancy of the autumnal
foliage.   Here indeed decay is beautiful; and nature appears more gorgeously clad in this her
fading mantle, than in all the summer's flush of
bloom in our less favoured climates. †   I noted

---

* This appears to me to be a most frequent ailment among
the American ladies : they must have particularly bilious constitutions.   I never remember travelling in a steam-boat, on
the smoothest water, without seeing sundry " afflicted fair
ones" who complained bitterly of *sea-sickness* in the river.

† In spite of its beauty, or rather on that very account,
an American autumn is to me particularly sad.   It presents

several beautiful wild flowers growing among the underwood; some of which I have seen adorning with great dignity our most cultivated gardens.* None of the trees had any size or appearance of age: they are the second growth, which have sprung from the soil once possessed by a mightier race of vegetables.   The quantity of mere underwood, and the number of huge black stumps rising in every direction a foot or two from the soil, bear witness to the existence of fine forest timber. The few cottages and farm houses which we passed reminded me of similar dwellings in France and Ireland; yet the peasantry here have not the same excuse for disorder and dilapidation as either the Irish or French.   The farms had the same deso-

---

an union of beauty and decay, that for ever reminds me of that loveliest disguise death puts on, when the cheek is covered with roses, and the eyes are like stars, and the life is perishing away; even so appear the gorgeous colours of the withering American woods. 'T is a whole forest dying of consumption.

* The magnolia and azalia are two of these; and, earlier in the summer, the whole country looks like fairy-land, with the profuse and lovely blossoms of the wild laurel, an evergreen shrub unequalled for its beauty, and which absolutely over-runs every patch of uncultivated ground. I wonder none of our parks have yet been adorned with it: it is a hardy plant, and I should think would thrive admirably in England.

late, untidy, untended look : the gates broken, the fences carelessly put up, or ill repaired ; the farming utensils sluttishly scattered about a littered yard, where the pigs seemed to preside by undisputed right; house-windows broken, and stuffed with paper or clothes; dishevelled women, and barefooted, anomalous looking human young things;—none of the stirring life and activity which such places present in England and Scotland; above all, none of the enchanting mixture of neatness, order, and rustic elegance and comfort, which render so picturesque the surroundings of a farm, and the various belongings of agricultural labour in my own dear country.*   The fences struck me

---

* In the opening chapter of that popular work, Eugene Aram, are the following words : — " It has been observed, and there is a world of homely, ay, and of legislative knowledge in the observation, that wherever you see a flower in a cottage garden, or a bird-cage at the window, you may feel sure that the cottagers are better and wiser than their neighbours." The truth of this observation is indisputable. But for such " humble tokens of attention to something beyond the *sterile labour* of life " you look in vain during a progress through this country. In New England alone, neatness and a certain endeavour at rustic elegance and adornment, in the cottages and country residences, recall those of their father-land; and the pleasure of the traveller is immeasurably heightened by this circumstance. If the wild beauties of uncultivated nature lead our contemplations to our great Maker, these lowly witnesses of the industry and natural refinement of

as peculiar; I never saw any such in England. They are made of rails of wood placed horizontally, and meeting at obtuse angles, so forming a zig-zag wall of wood, which runs over the country like the herring-bone seams of a flannel petticoat. At each of the angles two slanting stakes, considerably higher than the rest of the fence, were driven into the ground, crossing each other at the top, so as to secure the horizontal rails in their position.*   There was every now and then a soft

---

the laborious cultivator of the soil warm our heart with sympathy for our kind, and the cheering conviction that, however improved by cultivation, the sense of beauty, and the love of what is lovely, have been alike bestowed upon all our race; 't is a wholesome conviction, which the artificial divisions of society too often cause us to lose sight of.   The labourer, who, after "sweating in the eye of Phœbus" all the day, at evening trains the fragrant jasmine round his lowly door, is the very same man who, in other circumstances, would have been the refined and liberal patron of those arts which reflect the beauty of nature.

* In all my progress I looked in vain for the refreshing sight of a hedge — no such thing was to be seen; and their extreme rarity throughout the country renders the more cultivated parts of it arid-looking and comparatively dreary. These crooked fences in the south, and stone walls to the north, form the divisions of the fields, instead of those delicious "hedge-rows green," where the old elms delight to grow, where the early violets and primroses first peep sheltered forth, where the hawthorn blossoms sweeten the sum-

vivid strip of turf, along the road-side, that made me long for a horse.   Indeed the whole road would have been a delightful ride, and was a most bitter drive.   At the end of fourteen miles we turned into a swampy field, the whole fourteen coachfuls of us, and, by the help of Heaven, bag and baggage were packed into the coaches which stood on the rail-way ready to receive us.   The carriages were not drawn by steam, like those on the Li-

---

mer, the honeysuckle hangs its yellow garlands in the autumn, and the red " hips and haws " shine like bushes of earthly coral in the winter.

But the Americans are in too great a hurry to plant hedges : they have abundance of native material ; but a wooden fence is put up in a few weeks, a hedge takes as many years to grow ; and, as I said before, an American has not time to be a year about any thing. When first the country was settled, the wood was an encumbramce, and it was cut down accordingly ; that is by no means the case now ; and the only recommendation of these fences is, therefore, the comparative rapidity with which they can be constructed. One of the most amiable and distinguished men of this country once remarked to me, that the Americans were in too great a hurry about every thing they undertook to bring any thing to perfection. And certainly, as far as my observation goes, I should *calculate* that an American is born, lives, and dies twice as fast as any other human creature. I believe one of the great inducements to this national hurry is, that " time is money," which is true ; but it is also true, sometimes, that " most haste makes worst speed."

verpool rail-way, but by horses, with the mere advantage in speed afforded by the iron ledges, which,
to be sure, compared with our previous progress
through the ruts, was considerable.   Our coachful
got into the first carriage of the train, escaping,
by way of especial grace, the dust which one's
predecessors occasion.   This vehicle had but two
seats, in the usual fashion; each of which held
four of us.   The whole inside was lined with blazing
scarlet leather, and the windows *shaded* with stuff
curtains of the same refreshing colour; which,
with full complement of passengers, on a fine,
sunny, American summer's day, must make as
pretty a little miniature hell as may be, I should
think.   The baggage waggon, which went before
us, a little obstructed the view.   The road was
neither pretty nor picturesque; but still fringed
on each side with the many-coloured woods, whose
rich tints made variety even in sameness.   This
rail-road is an infinite blessing; 't is not yet finished,
but shortly will be so, and then the whole of that
horrible fourteen miles will be performed in comfort and decency in less than half the time.   In
about an hour and a half we reached the end of
our rail-road part of the journey, and found another steam-boat waiting for us, when we all embarked on the Delaware.   Again, the enormous
width of the river struck me with astonishment

and admiration. Such huge bodies of water mark out the country through which they run, as the future abode of the most extensive commerce, and greatest maritime power in the universe. The banks presented much the same features as those of the Raritan, though they were not quite so flat, and more diversified with scattered dwellings, villages, and towns. We passed Bristol and Burlington, stopping at each of them to take up passengers.* I sat working, having finished my book, not a little discomfited by the pertinacious staring of some of my fellow-travellers. One woman, in particular, after wandering round me in every direction, at last came and sat down opposite me, and literally gazed me out of countenance. One improvement they have adopted on board these boats is to forbid smoking, except in the fore part of the vessel. I wish they would suggest that, if the gentlemen would refrain from spitting about too, it would be highly agreeable to the female part of the community. The universal practice here of this disgusting trick makes me absolutely sick: every place is made a perfect piggery of—

---

* These are two very pretty villages of Quaker origin; situated in the midst of a fertile and lovely country, and much resorted to during the summer season by the Philadelphians.

street, stairs, steam-boat, every where—and behind
the scenes; and on the stage at rehearsal I have
been shocked and annoyed beyond expression by
this horrible custom. To-day, on board the boat,
it was a perfect shower of saliva all the time; and
I longed to be released from my fellowship with
these very obnoxious chewers of tobacco.* At
about four o'clock we reached Philadelphia, having
performed the journey between that and New York
(a distance of a hundred miles) in less than ten
hours, in spite of bogs, ruts, and all other impe-
diments. The manager came to look after us and
our goods, and we were presently stowed into a
coach which conveyed us to the Mansion House,
the best reputed inn in Philadelphia. On asking
for our bed-rooms, they showed D—— and myself
into a double-bedded room. On my remonstrating
against this, the chamber-maid replied, that they
were not accustomed to allow lodgers so *much room*

* It has happened to me after a few hours' travelling in a
steam-boat to find the white dress, put on fresh in the morning, covered with yellow tobacco stains; nor is this very
offensive habit confined to the lower orders alone. I have seen
gentlemen spit upon the carpet of the room where they were
sitting, in the company of women, without the slightest remorse; and I remember once seeing a gentleman, who was
travelling with us, very deliberately void his tobacco juice
into the bottom of the coach, instead of through the windows, to my inexpressible disgust.

as a room apiece. However, upon my insisting,. they gave me a little nest just big enough to turn about in, but where, at least, I can be by myself. Dressed, and dined at five; after dinner, wrote journal till tea-time, and then came to bed.

Tuesday, 9th.

Rose at half-past eight. Went and took a bath. On my way thither, drove through two melancholy looking squares, which reminded me a little of poor old Queen Square in Bristol. The ladies' baths were closed, but as I was not particular, they gave me one in the part of the house usually allotted to the men's use. I was much surprised to find two baths in one room, but it seems to me that the people of this country have an aversion to solitude, whether eating, sleeping, or under any other circumstances.

  * * * * *

  * * * * *

I made acquaintance with a bewitching Newfoundland puppy whom I greatly coveted. Came home, dressed, and breakfasted. After breakfast, righted my things, and wrote journal. Took a walk with my father through some of the principal streets The town is perfect silence and solitude, compared with New York; there is a greater air of age about it too, which pleases me. The red houses are not so fiercely red, nor the white facings so glaringly white; in short, it has not so new and flaunting a look, which is a great recommendation to me. The city is regularly built, the streets intersecting each other at right angles. We passed one or two pretty buildings in pure white marble, and the bank in Chestnut Street, which is a beautiful little copy of the Parthenon. The pure, cold, clear-looking marble, suits well with the severe and un-adorned style of architecture; and is in harmony, too, with the extreme brilliancy of the sky, and clearness of the atmosphere of this country.* We

---

* I wish that somebody would be so obliging as to impress people in general with the extreme excellence of a perception of the *fitness of things*. Besides the intrinsic beauty of works of art, they have a beauty derived from their appropriateness to the situations in which they are placed, and their harmony with the objects which surround them : this minor species of beauty is yet a very great one. If it were more studied, and better understood, public buildings would no longer appear as if they had fallen out of the clouds by chance ; parks and plantations would no more have the appearance of nurseries, where the trees were classed by kind, instead of being massed according to their various forms and colours ; and Gothic and classic edifices would not so often seem as if they had for-saken their appropriate situations, to rear themselves in climates, and among scenery, with which they in no way har-monise.

passed another larger building, also a bank, in the
Corinthian style, which did not please me so much.
The shops here are much better looking than those
at New York : the windows are larger, and more
advantageously constructed for the display of
goods; and there did not appear to be the same
anomalous mixture of vendibles, as in the New
York shops. The streets were very full of men
hurrying to the town house, to give their votes.
It is election time, and much excitement subsists
with regard to the choice of the future President.*

* Politics of all sorts, I confess, are far beyond my limited
powers of comprehension. Those of this country, as far as
I have been able to observe, resolve themselves into two great
motives, — the aristocratic desire of elevation and separation,
and the democratic desire of demolishing and levelling.
Whatever may be the immediate cause of excitement or
discussion, these are the two master-springs to which they
are referable. Every man in America is a politician ; and
political events, of importance only because they betray the
spirit which would be called into play by more stirring occasions, are occurring incessantly, and keeping alive the interest which high and low alike take in the evolutions of
their political machine. Elections of state officers, elections
of civil authorities, all manner of elections (for America is
one perpetual contest for votes), are going on all the year
round; and whereas the politics of men of private stations
in other countries are kept quietly by them, and exhibited
only on occasions of general excitement, those of an American
are as inseparable from him as his clothes, and mix up with
his daily discharge of his commonest daily avocations. I was

The democrats or radicals are for the re-election of General Jackson, but the aristocratic party, which here at all events is the strongest, are in favour of H enry Clay. Here is the usual quantity of shouting and breaking windows that we are accustomed to on these occasions. I saw a caricature of Jackson and Van Buren, his chief supporter, which was entitled " The King and his Minister." Van Buren held a crown in his hand, and the devil was approaching Jackson with a sceptre. — Came in at half-past four, dressed for dinner : they gave us an excellent one. The master of this house was, it seems, once a man of independent fortune, and a great *bon vivant*. He has retained from thence a fellow-feeling for his guests, and does by

---

extremely amused at seeing over a hat shop in New York one day, " Anti-Bank Hat Store," written in most attractive characters, as an inducement for all good democrats to go in and purchase their beavers of so republican a hatter. The universal-suffrage system is of course the cause of this general political mania; and during an election of mayor or aldermen the good shopkeepers of New York are in as fierce a state of excitement as if the choice of a perpetual dictator were the question in point. Politics is the main subject of conversation among American men in society; but, as I said before, the immediate object of discussion being most frequently some petty local interest or other, strangers cannot derive much pleasure from, or feel much sympathy in, the debate.

them as he would be done by. After dinner, worked till tea-time; after tea, wrote journal, and now I'll go to bed. We are attended here by a fat old lively negro, by name Henry; who canters about in our behalf with great alacrity, and seems wrapt in much wonderment at many of our proceedings. By the by, the black who protected our baggage from the steam-boat was ycleped *Oliver Cromwell.* I have begun Grahame's History of America, and like it " mainly," as the old plays say.

Wednesday, 10*th.*

Rose at eight. After breakfast, trimmed a cap, and wrote to dear ——. The streets were in an uproar all night, people shouting and bonfires blazing; in short, electioneering fun, which seems to be pretty much the same all the world over. Clay has it hollow here, they say: I wonder what Colonel —— will say to that. At twelve o'clock, sallied forth with D—— to rehearsal. The theatre is very pretty; not large, but well sized, and I should think, favourably constructed for the voice.

*   *   *   *   *

*   *   *   *   *

Unless Aldabella is irresistibly lovely, as well as wicked, there is no accounting for the conduct

of Fazio.   My own idea of her, as well as Milman's
description, is every thing that can be conceived of
splendid in beauty, sparkling in wit, graceful in
deportment, gorgeous in apparel, and deep and
dangerous in crafty wiliness; in short, the old
serpent in the shape of Mrs. ———.   I wish Mrs.
——— would act that part: I could act it well
enough, but she would both act and look it, to the
very life.   After rehearsal, walked about the town
in quest of some *coques de perle* for my Bianca
dress: could not procure any.   I like this town
extremely: there is a look of comfort and cleanliness, and withal of age about it, which pleases
me.   It is quieter, too, than New York, and though
not so gay, for that very reason is more to my
fancy; the shops, too, have a far better appearance.
New York always gave me the idea of an irregular
collection of temporary buildings, erected for some
casual purpose, full of life, animation, and variety,
but not meant to endure for any length of time; a
fair, in short.   This place has a much more substantial, sober, and city-like appearance.   Came
home at half-past two.   In the hall met Mr. ———,
who is grown ten years younger since I saw him
last: it always delights me to see one of my fellow-
passengers, and I am much disappointed in not
finding ——— here.   Dined at three; after dinner,

read my father some of my journal ; went on with letter to ——, and then went and dressed myself. Took coffee, and adjourned to the theatre. The house was very full, but not so full as the Park on the first night of his acting in New York, which accounts for the greater stillness of the audience. I watched my father narrowly through his part to-night with great attention and some consequent fatigue, and the conclusion I have come to is this : that though his workmanship may be, and is, far finer *in the hand*, than that of any other artist I ever saw, yet its very minute accuracy and refinement renders it unfit for the frame in which it is exhibited. Whoever should paint a scene calculated for so large a space as a theatre, and destined to be viewed at the distance from which an audience beholds it, with the laborious finish and fine detail of a miniature, would commit a great error in judgment. Nor would he have the least right to complain, although the public should prefer the coarser, yet far more effective work of a painter, who, neglecting all refinement and niceness of execution, should merely paint with such full colouring, and breadth and boldness of touch, as to produce in the wide space he is called upon to fill, and upon the remote senses he appeals to, the *effect* of that which he intends to represent. Indeed he is the better artist of the two, though probably not the most intellectual man. For it is the part of such an one to know exactly what will best convey to the mass of mind and feeling to which he addresses himself the emotions and passions which he wishes them to experience.* Now the great

* I have often thought that the constant demand for small theatres, which I have heard made by persons of the higher classes of society in England, was a great proof of the decline of the more imaginative faculties among them; and the proportionate increase of that fastidious and critical spirit, which is so far removed from every thing which constitutes the essence of poetry. The idea of illusion in a dramatic exhibition is confined to the Christmas spectators of old tragedies and new pantomimes; the more refined portions of our English audiences yawn through Shakspeare's historical plays, and *quiz* through those which are histories of human nature and its awful passions. They have forgotten what human nature really is, and cannot even *imagine* it. They require absolute reality on the stage, because their incapable spirits scoff at poetical truth, and that absolute reality, in our days, consists in such representations as the Rent Day; or (crossing the water, for we dearly love what is foreign) the homely improbabilities of Victorine, Henriette, and a pack of equally worthless subjects of exhibition. Indeed, theatres have had an end; for the refined, the highly educated, the first classes of society, they have had an end; it will be long, however, before the mass is sufficiently refined to lose all power of imagination; and while our aristocracy patronise French melodramas, and seek their excitement in the most trashy sentimentalities of the modern *école romantique*, I have some hopes that our plebeian pits and galleries

beauty of all my father's performances, but particularly of Hamlet, is a wonderful accuracy in the
detail of the character which he represents; an
accuracy which modulates the emphasis of every
word, the nature of every gesture, the expression
of every look; and which renders the whole a
most laborious and minute study, toilsome in the
conception and acquirement, and most toilsome
in the execution. But the result, though the natural one, is not such as he expects, as the reward
of so much labour. Few persons are able to follow
such a performance with the necessary attention,
and it is almost as great an exertion to see it *un-
derstandingly*, as to act it. The amazing study of
it requires a study in those who are to appreciate
it, and, as I take it, this is far from being what the
majority of spectators are either capable or desir-
ous of doing; the actor loses his pains, and they
have but little pleasure. Those who perform, and
those who behold a play, have but a certain proportion of power of exciting, and capability of being excited. If, therefore, the actor expends his

---

may still retain their sympathy for the loves of Juliet and
the sorrows of Ophelia. I would rather a thousand times
act either of those parts to a set of Manchester mechanics,
than to the most select of our aristocracy, for they are " nothing, if not critical."

power of exciting, and his audience's power of being excited, upon the detail of the piece, and continues through five whole acts to draw from both, the main and striking points, those of strongest appeal, those calculated most to rouse at once, and gratify the emotions of the spectator, have not the same intensity or vigour that they would have had, if the powers of both actor and audience had been reserved to give them their fullest effect. A picture requires light and shadow; and the very relief that throws some of the figures in a fine painting into apparent obscurity, in reality enhances the effect produced by those over which the artist has shed a stronger light. Every note in the most expressive song does not require a peculiar expression; and an air sung with individual emphasis on each note would be utterly unproductive of the desired effect. All things cannot have all their component parts equal, and " nothing pleaseth but rare accidents." This being so, I think that acting the best which skilfully husbands the actor's and spectator's powers, and puts forth the whole of the one, to call forth the whole of the other, occasionally only; leaving the intermediate parts sufficiently level, to allow him and them to recover the capability of again producing, and again receiving, such impressions. It

is constant that our finest nerves deaden and dull
from over-excitement, and require repose, before
they regain their acute power of sensation. At
the same time, I am far from advocating that most
imperfect conception and embodying of a part
which Kean allows himself: literally acting de-
tached passages alone, and leaving all the others,
and the entire character, indeed, utterly destitute
of unity, or the semblance of any consistency whatever. But Kean and my father are immediately
each other's antipodes, and in adopting their different styles of acting, it is evident that each has
been guided as much by his own physical and intellectual individuality, as by any fixed principle
of art. The one, Kean, possesses particular physical qualifications; an eye like an orb of light, a
voice, exquisitely touching and melodious in its
tenderness, and in the harsh dissonance of vehement passion terribly true; to these he adds the
intellectual ones of vigour, intensity, amazing
power of concentrating effect: these give him an
entire mastery over his audience in all striking,
sudden, impassioned passages; in fulfilling which,
he has contented himself, leaving unheeded what
he probably could not compass, the unity of conception, the refinement of detail, and evenness of

execution.* My father possesses certain physical defects, a faintness of colouring in the face and eye, a weakness of voice ; and the corresponding intellectual deficiencies, a want of intensity, vigour, and concentrating power: these circumstances have led him (probably unconsciously) to give his attention and study to the finer and more fleeting shades of character, the more graceful and delicate manifestations of feeling, the exquisite variety of all minor parts, the classic keeping of a highly wrought whole ; to all these, polished and refined tastes, an acute sense of the beauty of harmonious

---

* Kean is gone — and with him are gone Othello, Shylock, and Richard. I have lived among those whose theatrical creed would not permit them to acknowledge him as a great actor ; but they must be bigoted, indeed, who would deny that he was a great genius, a man of most original and striking powers, careless of art, perhaps because he did not need it ; but possessing those rare gifts of nature, without which art alone is as a dead body. Who that ever heard will ever forget the beauty, the unutterable tenderness of his reply to Desdemona's entreaties for Cassio, " Let him come when he will, I can deny thee nothing ; " the deep despondency of his " Oh, now farewell ; " the miserable anguish of his " Oh, Desdemona, away, away" ? Who that ever saw will ever forget the fascination of his dying eyes in Richard : when deprived of his sword, the wondrous power of his look seemed yet to avert the uplifted arm of Richmond. If he was irregular and unartist-like in his performances, so is Niagara, compared with the water-works of Versailles.

proportions, and a native grace, gentleness, and refinement of mind and manner, have been his prompters; but they cannot inspire those startling and tremendous bursts of passion, which belong to the highest walks of tragedy, and to which he never gave their fullest expression. I fancy my aunt Siddons united the excellences of both these styles. But to return to my father's Hamlet: every time I see it, something strikes me afresh in the detail. Nothing in my mind can exceed the exquisite beauty of his last " Go on — I follow thee," to the ghost. The full gush of deep and tender faith, in spite of the awful mystery, to whose unfolding he is committing his life, is beautiful beyond measure. It is distinct, and wholly different from the noble, rational, philosophic conviction, " And for my soul, what can it do to that?" It is full of the unutterable fondness of a believing heart, and brought to my mind, last night, those holy and lovely words of scripture, " Perfect love casteth out fear:" it enchanted me.* There is

---

* I have acted Ophelia three times with my father, and each time, in that beautiful scene where his madness and his love gush forth together like a torrent swollen with storms, that bears a thousand blossoms on its troubled waters, I have experienced such deep emotion as hardly to be able to speak. The exquisite tenderness of his voice, the wild compassion and forlorn pity of his looks, bestowing that on others,

one thing in which I do not believe my father ever has been, or ever will be, excelled; his high and noble bearing, his gallant, graceful, courteous deportment; his perfect good-breeding on the stage; unmarked alike by any peculiarity of time, place, or self (except peculiar grace and beauty). He appears to me the beau ideal of the courtly, thorough-bred, chivalrous gentleman from the days of the admirable Crichton down to those of George the Fourth. Coming home after the play, the marble buildings in the full moonlight reminded me of the Ghost in Hamlet: they looked like pale majestic spirits, cold, calm, and colourless.

Thursday, 11*th.*

Rose rather late. After breakfast, wrote journal;

---

which, above all others, he most needed; the melancholy restlessness, the bitter self-scorning; every shadow of expression and intonation was so full of all the mingled anguish that the human heart is capable of enduring, that my eyes scarce fixed on his ere they filled with tears; and long before the scene was over, the letters and jewel cases I was tendering·to him were wet with them. The hardness of professed actors and actresses is something amazing: after acting this part, I could not but recall the various Ophelias I have seen, and commend them for the astonishing absence of every thing like feeling which they exhibited. Oh, it made my heart sore to act it.

at twelve, went to rehearsal.　　＊　　＊　　＊

＊　　＊　　＊　　＊　　＊

After rehearsal, came home, habited, and went to the riding-school to try some horses. *Merci de moi !* what quadrupeds ! How they did wallop and shamble about ; poor half-broken dumb brutes ! they know no better ; and as the natives here are quite satisfied with their shuffling, rollicking, mongrel pace, half trot, half canter, why it is not worth while to break horses in a christian-like fashion for them.＊ I found something that I think my father can ride with tolerable comfort, but must go

---

＊ I am speaking now only of the common saddle-horses that one sees about the streets and roads. The southern breed of race-horses is a subject of great interest and care to all sporting men here : they are very beautiful animals, of a remarkably slight and delicate make. But the perfection of horses in this county are those trained for trotting : their speed is almost incredible. I have been whirled along in a light-built carriage by a pair of famous professed trotters, who certainly got over the ground at the rate of a moderate going steam-engine, and this without ever for a moment breaking into a gallop. The fondness of the Americans for this sort of horses, however, is one reason why one can so rarely obtain a well mouthed riding-horse. These trotters are absolutely carried on the bit, and require only a snaffle, and an arm of iron to hold them up. A horse well set upon his haunches is not to be met with ; and owing to this mode of breaking, their action is entirely from the head and shoulders ; and they both look and feel as if they would tumble down on their noses.

again to-morrow and see after something for my-self.   Came home: the enchanting Mr. Head has allowed me a piano-forte; but in bringing it into the room, the stupid slave broke one of its legs off, whereat I was like to faint, for I thought Mr. Head would wish me hanged therefore.   Nothing can exceed the civility of the people here, and the house is extremely well kept, quiet, and comfort-able. Came home in high delight with this Quaker city, which is indeed very pretty and pleasant. Played on the piano: dressed for dinner.   After, dinner, practised till tea-time, finished journal, discussed metaphysics with D——, for which I am a fool; wrote to-day's journal, and now to bed. I have a dreadful cold and cough, and have done nothing but hack and snivel the whole day long : this is a bad preparation for to-morrow's work. Howsoever ——

Friday, 12*th.*

Rose at eight.   After breakfast, sat writing jour-nal and letter to ——.   At half-past eleven, went to rehearsal.   Afterwards walked down to the riding-school with my father. The horse I was to look at had not arrived; but my father saw the grey.   We were there for some time; and during that whole some time a tall, thin, unhappy looking gentleman, who had gotten up upon a great hulking rawboned horse, kept trotting round and round, with his legs dangling down, *sans* stirrups, at the rate of a mile and a quarter an hour; occasionally ejaculating in the mildest of tones, " keome — keome up ;" whereat the lively brute, nothing persuaded, proceeded in the very same pace, at the very same rate; and this went on till I wondered at the man and the beast. Came home and put out things for the theatre. My cold and cough are dreadful. After dinner, practised: invented and executed a substitute for the *coques de perle* in my Bianca dress; and lay down to rest a little before my work. At six, went to the theatre: the house was very full; and D—— and my father say that I was extremely ungracious in my acknowledgment of their greeting. I cannot tell; I did not mean to be so; I made them three courtesies, and what could woman do more? Of course, I can neither feel nor look so glad to see them, as I am to see my own dear London people: neither can I be as profound in my obeisance, as when my audience is civil enough to rise to me: " there is differences, look you."   *   *   *

    *   *   *   *   *

    *   *   *   *   *

My Fazio had a pair of false black whiskers on, which distilled a black stripe of trickling cement down his cheeks, and kept me in agony every time he had to embrace me. My voice was horrible to hear; alternately like Mrs. —— and ——, and every now and then it was all I could do to utter at all. This audience is the most unapplausive I ever acted to, not excepting my *excitable* friends north of the Tweed. They were very attentive, certainly, but how they did make me work! 'T is amazing how much an audience loses by this species of hanging back, even where the silence proceeds from unwillingness to interrupt a good performance: though in reality it is the greatest compliment an actor can receive, yet he is deprived by that very stillness of half his power. Excitement is reciprocal between the performer and the audience: he creates it in them, and receives it back again from them; and in that last scene in Fazio, half the effect that I produce is derived from the applause which I receive, the very noise and tumult of which tends to heighten the nervous energy which the scene itself begets. I know that my aunt Siddons has frequently said the same thing. And besides the above reason for applause, the physical powers of an actor require, after any tremendous exertion, the rest and regathering of breath and strength, which the interruption of the audience affords him; moreover, as 't is the conventional mode of expressing approbation in a theatre, it is chilling and uncomfortable to go toiling on, without knowing whether, as the maid-servants say, " one gives satisfaction or no." They made noise enough, however, at the end of the play. Came home, supped, and to bed: weary to death, and with a voice like a cracked bagpipe.

Saturday, 13*th.*

Rose at half-past eight. After breakfast, wrote journal; practised for an hour; got things ready for to-morrow; put on my habit, which I had no sooner done than the perverse clouds began to rain. The horses came at two, but the weather was so bad that I sent them away again. Practised for another hour, read a canto in Dante, and dressed for dinner. After dinner, worked and practised. Came to my own room, and tried to scribble something for the Mirror, at my father's request; the editors having made an especial entreaty to him, that I might write something for them, and also sit to some artist for them. I could not accomplish any thing, and they must just take something that I have by me: as for my

physiognomy, that they shall certainly not have
with my own good leave.   I will never expend so
much useless time again as to sit for my picture;
nor will I let any unhappy painter again get abused
for painting me as I am, which is any thing but
what I look like.   Lawrence alone could do it:
there is no other that could see my spirit through
my face; and as for the face without that, the less
that is seen of it the better.   Came down to tea,
and found a young gentleman sitting with my
father; one Mr. ——.   *   *   *

   *   *   *   *   *

   *   *   *   *   *

He was a pretty-spoken, *genteel* youth enough: he
drank tea with us, and offered to ride with me.
He is, it seems, a great fortune; consequently, I
suppose (in spite of his inches), a great man.
Now I 'll go to bed: my cough 's enough to kill a
horse.

Sunday, 14*th*.

Rose late; so late that, by the time I had breakfasted, it was no longer time to go to church.

   *   *   *   *   *

   *   *   *   *   *

Finished my first letter to ——.   Mr. —— called,

and told us that he was going about *agitating*, and that Jackson was certainly to be re-elected.   *

*   *   *   *   *

*   *   *   *   *

At three o'clock D—— and I sallied forth to go to church. Following the silver voices of the Sabbath bells, as they called the worshippers to the house of prayer, we entered a church with a fine simple façade, and found ourselves in the midst of a Presbyterian congregation. 'T is now upwards of eight years since, a school girl, I used to attend a dissenter's chapel. The form of worship, though displeasing to me in itself, borrowed a charm to-day from old association.   How much of the past it did recall !   *   *

*   *   *   *   *

*   *   *   *   *

Came home and dressed for dinner.   After dinner half-killed myself with laughter over an Irish version of Fazio, ycleped Grimaldi, from which the author swears Milman has shamefully filched the plot, characters, and even the language, I believe, of his drama. A gentleman of the press, by name ——, paid us an evening visit. He seems an intelligent young man enough; and when he spoke of the autumnal woods, by the Oneida lake, his expressions were poetical and enthusiastic;

and he pleased me.*   He seems to think much of
having had the honour of corresponding with
sundry of the small literati of London. *Je lui
en fais mon compliment.*   When he was gone,
wrote another letter to ——, journal, and now
to bed.

Monday, 15*th.*

Rose at eight ; took a hot bath. The more I
read of Grahame, the better I like him and his
history. Those early settlers in Massachusetts

---

* Except where they have been made political tools,
newspaper writers and editors have never, I believe, been
admitted into good society in England.   It is otherwise
here : newspapers are the main literature of America; and I
have frequently heard it quoted, as a proof of a man's abilities, that he writes in such and such a newspaper. Besides
the popularity to be obtained by it, it is often attended with
no small literary consideration ; and young men here, with
talents of a really high order, and who might achieve far
better things, too often are content to accept this very
mediocre mode of displaying their abilities, at very little
expense of thought or study, and neglect far worthier objects
of ambition, and the rewards held out by a distant and per-
manent fame. I know that half my young gentlemen acquaintance here would reply, that they must live in the
mean time, and it is a real and deep evil, arising from the
institutions of this country, that every man must toil from
day to day for his daily bread ; and in this degrading and
spirit-loading care, all other nobler desires are smothered.
It is a great national misfortune.

were fine fellows, indeed; and Cotton, one of the
finest samples of a Christian priest imaginable.
After breakfast, went to rehearsal. The day was
cold, but beautifully bright and clear. The pure,
fresh, invigorating air, and gay sunlight, together
with the delightfully clean streets, and pretty
mixture of trees and buildings in this nice town,
caused me to rejoice, as I walked along.* After
rehearsal, saw Sinclair and his wife. So — we are
to act the Gamester here. Went and ordered a
dress for that same, my own being at New York.
Came home, put out things for the theatre, practised an hour; dined at three. After dinner, read
a canto in Dante: he is my admiration!—great,
great master!—a philosopher profound, as all
poets should be; a glorious poet, as I wish all
philosophers were. Sketched till dark. Chose a
beautiful claret-coloured velvet for Mrs. Beverley;
which will cost Miss Kemble eleven guineas, by
this living light. At six, went to the theatre. I
never beheld any thing more gorgeous than the sky

---

* This delightful virtue of neatness is carried almost to an
inconvenient pitch by the worthy Philadelphians: the town,
every now and then, appears to be in a perfect frenzy of
cleanliness; and of a Saturday morning, early, the streets
are really impassable, except to a good swimmer. " Cleanliness," says the old saw, " is near to godliness." Philadelphia must be very near heaven.

at sunset.   Autumn is an emperor here, clothed in crimson and gold, and canopied with ruddy glowing skies.   Yet I like the sad russet cloak of our own autumnal woods; I like the sighing voice of his lament through the vaporous curtain that rises round his steps; I like the music of the withered leaves that rustle in his path; and oh, above all, the solemn thoughts that wait upon him, as he goes stripping the trees of their bright foliage, leaving them like the ungarlanded columns of a deserted palace.   The play was Romeo and Juliet.   My father was the " youngest of that name," for want of a better, or, rather, of a worse. How beautiful this performance must have been, when the youthful form made that appear natural which now seems the triumph of art over nature. Garrick said, that to act Romeo required a grey head upon green shoulders.   Indeed, 'tis difficult!   Oh, that our sapient judges did but know half how difficult.   It is delightful to act with my father.   One's imagination need toil but little, to see in him the very thing he represents; whereas, with all other Romeos, although they were much younger men, I have had to do double work with that useful engine, my fancy: first, to get rid of the material obstacle staring me in the face, and then to substitute some more congenial representative of that sweetest vision of youth and love. Once, only, this was not necessary.

*　　　*　　　*　　　*　　　*

*　　　*　　　*　　　*　　　*

The audience here are, without exception, the most disagreeable I ever played to.　Not a single hand did they give the balcony scene, or my father's scene with the friar: they are literally immovable.　They applauded vehemently at the end of my draught scene, and a great deal at the end of the play; but they are, nevertheless, intolerably dull; and it is all but impossible to act to them.　　*　　　*　　　*　　　*

*　　　*　　　*　　　*　　　*

*　　　*　　　*　　　*　　　*

The man who acted Capulet did it better than any Capulet I ever acted with ; and the nurse, besides looking admirably, acted her part very well : and 't is hard to please me, after poor dear old Mrs. Davenport.　The house was literally crammed from floor to ceiling.　Came home tired and hoarse ; though my voice was a good deal better to-day.　Mr. —— supped with us.　My father expected a visit from the haggling Boston manager, and chose to have a witness to the conference.

Tuesday, 16th.

Rose at nine. After breakfast, read a canto in Dante; wrote journal; practised for an hour. The Boston manager, it seems, does not approve of our terms; and after bargaining till past two o'clock last night with my father, the latter, wearied out with his illiberal trafficking, and coarse vulgarity of manner, declined the thing altogether: so, unless the gentleman thinks better of the matter, we shall not go to Boston this winter.* At one o'clock, habited; and at two, rode out with my father. The day was most enchanting, mild, bright, and sunny; but the roads were deplorable, and the country utterly dull. My horse was a hard-mouthed, half-broken beast, without pace of any christian kind soever; a perfect rack on hoofs: how it did jog and jumble me. However, my bones are young, and my courage good, and I don't mind a little hard work; but the road was

---

* The final result of our very unfortunate dealings with this gentleman is, that our earnings (and they are not lightly come by), to the amount of near three thousand dollars, are at this moment in the hands of a trustee, and Heaven and a New England court of justice will decide whether they are ever to come into ours.

so villanously bad, and the surrounding country
so weary, dull, stale, and unprofitable, that I was
heartily sick of my ride, when we turned towards
Fairmount, the site of some large water-works on
the Schuylkill, by which Philadelphia is supplied
with water. On our right I descried, over some
heights, a castellated building of some extent,
whose formidable appearance, at least, bespoke an
arsenal; but it was the entrance to the peniten-
tiary instead: and presently the river, bright,
and broad, and placid as a lake, with its beautiful
banks, and rainbow-tinted woods, opened upon us.
We crossed a covered wooden bridge, and followed the water's edge. The rich colours of the
foliage cast a warm light over the transparent face
of the mirror-like stream; and, far along the
winding shores, a mingled mantle of gorgeous-
glowing tints lay over the woody banks, and was
reflected in the still, sunny river. Indeed, it was
lovely! But our time was growing short, and we
had to turn home; which we did by a pleasant
and more direct path. My horse, towards the
end of the ride, got more manageable; and I
doubt whether it would not be wiser to continue
to ride it than try another, which may be just as
bad, and, moreover, a *stranger*. My riding-cap
seemed to excite universal marvel wherever we

passed. We came in at five o'clock; dressed, and dined. Just as I had finished dinner, a most beautiful, fragrant, and delicious nosegay was brought to me, with a very laconic note from a Philadelphia "*friend*," dashed under, as though from a Quaker. Whoever 't is from, Jew or Gentile, Puritan or Pagan, he, she, or it hath my most unbounded gratitude. Spent an ecstatic half hour in arranging my flowers in glasses; gave orders about my Mrs. Beverley's gown, and began marking journal; while doing so, a card was brought up.   *   *   *

     *   *   *   *   *

     *   *   *   *   *

Presently Mr. —— came in, another of our Pacific fellow-sailors. It pleases me to see them : they seem to bring me nearer to England. He gave a dreadful account of his arrival in Baltimore, and of the state to which the cholera had reduced that city. Mr. —— amused me, by telling me that he had heard my behaviour canvassed with much censure by some man or other, who met me at Mr. ——, and who was horrified at my taking up a book, and then a newspaper; and, in short, being neither tragical nor comical, at a dinner-party. Of course, I must seem a very strange

animal to them all; but they seem just as strange
to me.   *   *   *   *

*   *   *   *   *

Wednesday, 17*th*.

Rose at eight.   After breakfast, put out things
for the theatre.   At eleven, went to rehearsal.   It
seems there has been fighting, and rushing, and
tearing of coats at the box-office; and one man
has made forty dollars by purchasing and reselling
tickets at an increased price.   After rehearsal,
came home.   Mr. —— called, and sat some time :
he sails for England on the twenty-fourth.   England, oh England ! — yet, after all, what is there
in that name?   It is not my home; it is not those
beloved ones whose fellowship is half the time
what we call *home.*   Is it really and truly the
yearning of the roots for the soil in which they
grew?   Perhaps it is only the restless roving
spirit, that still would be where it is not.   I know
not.   His description of American life and manners (and he knows both, for he has lived constantly in this country, and his partialities are, I
believe, fairly divided between it and his own,) is
any thing but agreeable.   *   *

*   *   *   *   *

K 5

The dignified and graceful influence which married women, among us, exercise over the tone of manners, uniting the duties of home to the charms of social life, and bearing, at once, like the orange-tree, the fair fruits of maturity with the blossoms of their spring, is utterly unknown here. Married women are either house-drudges and nursery-maids, or, if they appear in society, comparative ciphers; and the retiring, modest, youthful bearing, which among us distinguishes girls of fifteen or sixteen, is equally unknown. Society is entirely led by chits, who in England would be sitting behind a pinafore; the consequence is, that it has neither the elegance, refinement, nor the propriety which belongs to ours; but is a noisy, rackety, vulgar congregation of flirting boys and girls, alike without style or decorum.* When

* When we arrived in America, we brought letters of introduction to several persons in New York: many were civil enough to call upon us: we were invited out to sundry parties, and were introduced into what is there called the first society. I do not wish to enter into any description of it, but will only say that I was most disagreeably astonished; and had it been my fate to have passed through the country as rapidly as most travellers do, I should have carried away a very unfavourable impression of the *best* society of New York. Fortunately, however, for me, my visits were repeated, and my stay prolonged; and, in the course of time, I became acquainted with many individuals whose manners

Mr. —— was gone, practised till dinner time. After dinner, practised for half an hour; marked

and acquirements were of a high order, and from whose in-tercourse I derived the greatest gratification. But they generally did me the favour to visit me; and I still could not imagine how it happened that I never met them at the parties to which I was invited, and in the circles where I visited. I soon discovered that they formed a society among them-selves, where all those qualities which I had looked for among the self-styled *best* were to be found. When I name Miss Sedgwick, Halleck, Irving, Bryant, Paulding, and some of less fame, but whose acquirements rendered their com-panionship delightful indeed, amongst whom I felt proud and happy to find several of my own name, it will no longer appear singular that they should feel too well satisfied with the resources of their own society, either to mingle in that of the vulgar *fashionables*, or seek with avidity the acquaint-ance of every stranger that arrives in New York. It is not to be wondered at that foreigners have spoken as they have of what is termed fashionable society here, or have con-demned, with unqualified censure, the manners and tone prevailing in it. Their condemnations are true and just as regards what they see; nor, perhaps, would they be much inclined to moderate them when they found that persons possessing every quality that can render intercourse between rational creatures desirable were held in light esteem, and neglected, as either bores, blues, or dowdies, by those so infinitely their inferiors in every worthy accomplishment. The same separation, or, if any thing, a still stronger one, sub-sists in Philadelphia between the self-styled fashionables and the really good society. The distinction there is really of a nature perfectly ludicrous. A friend of mine was de-scribing to me a family whose manners were unexception-

journal, till time to go to the theatre; took coffee, and away. The house was crammed again, and the play better acted than I have ever seen it out of London, though Mrs. Candour had stuck upon her head a bunch of feathers which threatened the gods; and Lady Sneerwell had dragged all her

---

able, and whose mental accomplishments were of a high order: upon my expressing some surprise that I had never met with them, my informant replied, " Oh, no, they are not received by the Chestnut Street *set*." If I were called upon to define that society in New York and Philadelphia which ranks (by right of self-arrogation) as first and best, I should say it is a purely dancing society, where a fiddle is indispensable to keep its members awake; and where their brains and tongues seem, by common consent, to feel that they had much better give up the care of mutual entertainment to the feet of the parties assembled; and they judge well. Now, I beg leave clearly to be understood, there is another, and a far more desirable circle; but it is not the one into which strangers find their way generally. To an Englishman, this *fashionable* society presents, indeed, a pitiful sample of lofty pretensions without adequate foundation. Here is a constant endeavour to imitate those states of European society which have for their basis the feudal spirit of the early ages, and which are rendered venerable by their rank, powerful by their wealth, and refined, and in some degree respectable, by great and general mental cultivation. Of Boston, I have not spoken. The society there is of an infinitely superior order. A very general degree of information, and a much greater simplicity of manners, render it infinitely more agreeable. But of that hereafter.

hair off her face, which needed to be as pretty as it was, to endure such an exposure. I do not wonder the New Yorkians did not approve of my Lady Teazle. If, as —— tells me, Mrs. —— is their idea of the perfection of good-breeding, well may my delineation of a lady be condemned as " nothing particular." Yet I am sorry I must continue to lie under their censure, for I, unfortunately for myself, have seen ladies, " ripe and real," who, from all I can see, hear, and understand, differ widely from the good manners of their " beau ideal." The fact is, I am not " *genteel* " enough, and I am conscious of it. The play went off remarkably well. Came to bed at half-past eleven.   *   *   *   *

*   *   *   *   *

Thursday, 18*th.*

Here is the end of October, the very mourning-time of the year with us, and my room is full of flowers, and the sun is so bright and powerful, that it is impossible to go out with a shawl, or without a parasol. Went to rehearsal at twelve; at two, came in and habited; and at half-past two, rode out with my father. We took the road to the Schuylkill at once, through Arch Street, which is a fine, broad, long street, running parallel with Chestnut Street. We walked along the road under the intense sunlight that made all things look sleepy around. Turning between some rising banks, through a defile where the road wound up a hill, we caught a glimpse of a white house standing on the sunny slope of a green rise. The undulating grounds around were all bathed in warm light, relieved only by the massy shadows of the thick woods that sheltered them. It was a bit of England.   *   *   *   *

     *   *   *   *   *

Some good farming and tidy out-houses, and dependencies, completed the resemblance, and made me think that this must be the dwelling of some of my own country people. How can they live here? Here, even in the midst of what is fair and peaceful in nature, I think my home would haunt me, and the far off chiming of the waves against her white shores resound in my ears through the smooth flowing of the Schuylkill.* After pursuing

* The beautiful villas on the banks of the Schuylkill are all either utterly deserted and half ruinous, or let out by the proprietors to tavern keepers. The reason assigned for this is, that during that season of the year when it would be most desirable to reside there, the fever and ague takes possession of the place, and effectually banishes all other occupants. This very extraordinary and capricious malady is as

a level uninteresting road for some time, we turned
off to the right, and standing on the brow of a

---

uncertain in its residence, as unwelcome where it does fix its
abode. The courses of some of the rivers, and even whole
tracts of country away from the vicinity of the water, have
been desolated by it : from these it has passed away entirely,
and removed itself to other districts, before remarkably
healthy. Sometimes it visits particular places at intervals
of one or two seasons ; sometimes it attaches itself to one
side of a river, and leaves the inhabitants of the other in the
enjoyment of perfect health ; in short, it is quite as unac-
countable in its proceedings as a fine lady. Many causes
have been assigned as its origin; which, however, have
varied in credibility at almost every new appearance of the
malady. The enormous quantity of decaying vegetation
with which the autumn woods are strewn, year after year,
till it absolutely forms a second soil; the dam lately erected
by the water-works, and which, intercepting the tide, causes
occasional stagnation; the unwholesome action of water
lodging in hollows in the rocks ; are all reasons which have
been given to me when I have enquired about this terrible
nuisance along the banks of the Schuylkill: but there is
another, and one which appeared so obvious to me that
when first I saw it, I felt much inclined to attribute the
fever and ague to that, and to that alone. I allude to a foul
and stagnant ditch, lying between the tow-path and the
grounds of these country houses, of nearly a mile in length,
and of considerable width. When I saw the sun pouring its
intense light down into this muddy pool, covered with thick
and unwholesome incrustations, I could not help remarking
that this alone was quite sufficient to breed a malaria in the
whole neighbourhood ; and that if the gentlemen proprietors
of the lands along this part of the river would drain this
very poisonous looking repository for bull frogs, their dwellings would, in all probability, be free from fever and ague.

considerable declivity, had a most enchanting glimpse of the Schuylkill and its woody shores. The river makes a bend just above the water-works, and the curving banks scooping themselves form a lovely little sunny bay. It was more like a lake, just here, than a flowing stream. The sky was so blessedly serene, and the air so still, that the pure deep-looking water appeared to sleep, while the bright hues of the heavens, and the glowing tints of the woody shores, were mirrored with wondrous vividness on its bosom. I never saw such gorgeousness, and withal such perfect harmony of colouring. The golden sky, the mingled green, brown, yellow, crimson, and dark maroon, that clothed the thickets; the masses of grey granite, with the vivid, mossy green that clung round them; the sunny purple waters; the warm, red colour of the road itself, as it wound down below, with a border of fresh-looking turf on either side of it; the radiant atmosphere of rosy light that hung over all; all combined to present a picture of perfect enchantment. The eye was drunk with beauty.* How I thought of Mr. ——. Indeed a painter would have gone crazy over it,

* This beautiful younger world appears to me to have received the portion of the beloved younger son — the " coat of many colours."

and I, who am not a painter, was half crazy that
I was not. Though if I had been, what would it
have availed? Such colours are from God's pal-
let, and mortal hand may no more copy, than it
could mingle them. We rode on through scenery
of the same description, passing in our way a farm
and dairy, where the cattle were standing, not in
open pasture land, but in a corner of forest-ground,
all bright with the golden shedding of the trees;
it was very picturesque. A little runlet of water,
too, that held the middle of a tangled ravine, ran
glittering like a golden snake through the underwood, while the stems of the trees, and the light
foliage on the edge of the thick woody screens
were bathed in yellow sunshine. All around was
beautiful, and rich, and harmonious to the eye,
and should have been so to the spirit.   *   *

*   *   *   *   *

Returned home at about half-past five, dined at
six; found another beautiful nosegay waiting for
me, from my unknown furnisher of sweets. This
is almost as tantalising as it is civil; and I would
give half my lovely flowers to find out who sends
them to me. Distributed them all over the room,
and was as happy as a queen. Mr. —— called.
My father was obliged to go out upon business, so
D—— and I had to entertain that worthy youth.

He seems to have a wonderful veneration for a
parcel of scribblers whose names were never heard
of in England, beyond the limits of their own narrow coteries.   But he speaks like an enthusiast of
the woods and waters of his glorious country, and
I excuse his taste in poetry.   Now isn't this strange,
that a man who can feel the amazing might, majesty, and loveliness of nature, can endure for a moment the mawkish scribbling of these poetasters?
Verily, we be anomalous beasts.   *   *

*   *   *   *   *

AUTUMN.

Thou comest not in sober guise,
    In mellow cloak of russet clad —
Thine are no melancholy skies,
    Nor hueless flowers pale and sad;
But, like an emperor, triumphing,
    With gorgeous robes of Tyrian dyes,
Full flush of fragrant blossoming,
    And glowing purple canopies.
How call ye this the season's fall,
    That seems the pageant of the year,
Richer and brighter far than all
    The pomp that spring and summer wear?
Red falls the westering light of day
    On rock and stream and winding shore;
Soft woody banks and granite grey
    With amber clouds are curtained o'er;

The wide clear waters sleeping lie
  Beneath the evening's wings of gold,
And on their glassy breast the sky
  And banks their mingled hues unfold.
Far in the tangled woods, the ground
  Is strewn with fallen leaves, that lie
Like crimson carpets all around
  Beneath a crimson canopy.
The sloping sun with arrows bright
  Pierces the forest's waving maze;
The universe seems wrapt in light, —
  A floating robe of rosy haze.
Oh, Autumn! thou art here a king;
  And round thy throne the smiling hours
A thousand fragrant tributes bring
  Of golden fruits and blushing flowers.

Oh! not upon thy fading fields and fells
  In such rich garb doth Autumn come to thee,
My home! — but o'er thy mountains and thy dells
  His footsteps fall slowly and solemnly.
Nor flower nor bud remaineth there to him,
  Save the faint-breathing rose, that, round the year,
Its crimson buds and pale soft blossoms dim,
  In lowly beauty constantly doth wear.
O'er yellow stubble lands, in mantle brown,
  He wanders through the wan October light;
Still as he goeth, slowly stripping down
  The garlands green that were the spring's delight.
At morn and eve thin silver vapours rise
  Around his path; but sometimes at mid-day
He looks along the hills with gentle eyes,
  That make the sallow woods and fields seem gay.

Yet something of sad sov'reignty he hath —
   A sceptre crown'd with berries ruby red;
And the cold sobbing wind bestrews his path
   With wither'd leaves that rustle 'neath his tread;
And round him still, in melancholy state,
   Sweet solemn thoughts of death and of decay,
In slow and hush'd attendance, ever wait,
   Telling how all things fair must pass away.

Tuesday, 23d.

At ten o'clock, went to rehearsal. Rehearsed the Hunchback, and then Fazio: this is tolerably hard work, with acting every night: we don't steal our money, that's one comfort. Came home, found a letter for me in a strange hand.   *

*   *   *   *   *

Went on with my letter to —— : while doing so, was interrupted by the entrance of a strange woman, who sat herself down, apparently in much confusion. She told me a story of great distress, and claimed my assistance as a fellow-country-woman. I had not a farthing of money: D—— and my father were out; so I took the reference she gave me, and promised to enquire into her condition. The greatest evil arising from the many claims of this sort which are made upon us, wherever we go, is the feeling of distrust and suspicion which they engender, and the sort of excuse which they teach us to apply plausibly to our unwillingness to answer such demands. " Oh, ten to one, an impostor," is soon said, and instances enough may unfortunately be found to prove the probability of such a conclusion. Yet in this sweeping condemnation, one real case of misery may be included, and that possibility should make us pause, for 't is one that, if afterwards detected, may be the source of heavy condemnation, and bitter regret to ourselves. †   *   *   *   *

† This country is in one respect blessed above all others, and above all others deserving of blessing. There are no poor — I say there are none, there *need* be none ; none here need lift up the despairing voice of hopeless and helpless want, towards that Heaven which hears when men will not. No father here need work away his body's health, and his spirit's strength, in unavailing labour, from day to day, and from year to year, bowed down by the cruel curse his fellows lay upon him. No mother need wish, in the bitterness of her heart, that the children of her breast had died before they exhausted that nourishment which was the only one her misery could feel assured would not fail them. None need be born to vice, for none are condemned to abject poverty. Oh, it makes the heart sick to think of all the horrible anguish that has been suffered by thousands and thousands of those wretched creatures, whose want begets a host of moral evils fearful to contemplate ; whose existence begins in poverty, struggles on through care and toil, and heart-grinding burdens, and ends in destitution, in sickness, — alas ! too often in crime and infamy. Thrice blessed is this coun-

*   *   *   *   *

*   *   *   *   *

The fact is, that to give well, one should give equally one's trouble with one's money: the one in all cases, the other where one's enquiries are satisfactorily answered.—Received a purple bound, gilt-edged periodical, published at Boston, from Mr. ——.   *   *   *   *

*   *   *   *   *

*   *   *   *   - *

The literary part of the book seems much on a par with that of similar works in England, but there was a wide difference in the excellence of the engravings. There was one from that pretty picture, the Bride's Maid ; a coarse, bad engraving,

---

try, for no such crying evil exists in its bosom; no such moral reproach, no such political rottenness. Not only is the eye never offended with those piteous sights of human suffering, which make one's heart bleed, and whose number appals one's imagination in the thronged thoroughfares of the European cities; but the mind reposes with delight in the certainty that not one human creature is here doomed to suffer and to weep through life; not one immortal soul is thrown into jeopardy by the combined temptations of its own misery, and the heartless selfishness of those who pass it by without holding out so much as a finger to save it. If we have any faith in the excellence of mercy and benevolence, we must believe that this alone will secure the blessing of Providence on this country.

but yet how much of the sadness of the original
it recalled to me. It is a painful thing to look at :
it brings before one too much of the sorrow of life,
of the anguish that has been endured ; that is daily,
hourly, endured in this prison-house of torments.
After dinner, went on writing to ———, till time to
go to the theatre. The house was not as full as I
had expected, though a good one enough. My
father looked wonderfully well and young : there
is certainly some difference in acting with him, but
this part fatigues me horribly.

Wednesday, 24th.

Went to rehearsal at eleven ; at half-past one,
went with D——— to find out something about my
yesterday's poor woman. The worst of it is, that
my trouble involves necessarily the trouble of
somebody else, as I cannot go trotting and exploring about by myself. The references were
sufficiently satisfactory, that is, they proved that
she was poor, and in distress, and willing to work.
I gave her what I could, and the man by whom
she is employed seems anxious to afford her work ;
so I hope she will get on a little. The " God
bless you," of gratitude, even if uttered by guileful
and unworthy lips, is surely yet a blessing if it

alights on those who are seeking to do good. And if I were assured that that woman was the veriest impostor under the sun, I still should hope her prayer might descend with profit on my head; for I was sincere in my desire to do well by her. Came home, wrote a letter to ——, finished one to ——; and went to the theatre. It seems there have been,

> " Bloody noses and crack'd crowns,
> And all the currents of a heady fight,"

at the box-office, and truly the house bore witness thereto ; for it was crammed from floor to ceiling. The play was the Hunchback. I played very well, in spite of no green carpet, and no letter in the letter scene, which lost one of my favourite points ; one, by the by, that I am fond of, because it is all my own.   *   *   *
   *   *   *   *   *
   *   *   *   *   *

Thursday, 25th.

After breakfast, went to rehearsal. Came home, put out things for the theatre, made myself a belt; received a whole bundle of smart annuals from Mr. ——; spent some time in looking over their

engravings. My gown looked very handsome, but my belt was too small; had to make another. The house was good, but not great. I played only so-so: the fact is, it is utterly impossible to play to this audience at all. They are so immovable, such very stocks and stones, that one is fairly exhausted with labouring to excite them, before half one's work is done. *   *   *   *
*   *   *   *   *
*   *   *   *   *

AUTUMN SONG.

The merriest time of all the year
Is the time when the leaves begin to fall,
When the chestnut-trees turn yellow and sear,
And the flowers are withering one and all;

When the thick green sward is growing brown,
And the honeysuckle berries are red,
And the oak is shaking its acorns down,
And the dry twigs snap 'neath the woodman's tread.

The merriest dance that e'er was seen
Is the headlong dance of the whirling leaves,
And the rattling stubble that flies between
The yellow ranks of the barley sheaves.

The merriest song that e'er was heard
Is the song of the sobbing autumn wind;
When the thin bare boughs of the elm are stirr'd,
And shake the black ivy round them twined.

The merriest time of all the year
Is the time when all things fade and fall,
When the sky is bleak, and the earth is drear,
Oh, that's the merriest month of all.

Friday, 26th.

While I was dressing, D——, like a good
angel, came in with three letters from England
in her hand.   *   *   *   *
        *   *   *   *   *

The love of excellent friends is one of God's
greatest blessings, and deserves our utmost thankfulness.   The counsel of sound heads and the
affection of Christian spirits is a staff of support,
and a spring of rejoicing through life.   *
        *   *   *   *   *

A Mr., Mrs., and young Mr. ——, called upon
us: they are the only inhabitants of this good city
who have done us that honour.   *   *
        *   *   *   *   *

As soon as my father came in, we sallied forth
to see the giantess of a ship the Americans have
been building, to thresh us withal.   I hooked myself up to ——, and away we strode; D—— and
my father struggling after us, as best they might.
The day was most beautiful; bright, sunny, and
fresh.   After walking at an immense pace for some

time, we bethought us of looking for our *poursui-vants ;* but neither sign nor vestige appeared of them. We stood still and waited, and went on, and stood still again. —— looked foolish at me, and I foolish at him: at length we wisely agreed that they had probably made the best of their way to the Navy yard, and thither we proceeded. We found them, according to our expectations, waiting for us, and proceeded to enter the building where this lady of the seas was propped upon a hundred stays ; surrounded with scaffolding, with galleries running round from the floor to the ceiling. We went on deck ; in fact, the Pennsylvania has been boarded by the English in our person, before she sets foot on the sea. How I should like to see that ship launched ; how she will sweep down from her holdings, and settle to the water, as a swan before swimming out ! How the shores will resound with living voices, applauding her like a living creature ; how much of national pride, of anticipated triumph, will be roused in every heart, as her huge wings first unfold their shadow over the sea, and she moves abroad, the glory and the wonder of the deep ! How, if this ship should ever lie in an English harbour ? If I were an American on board of her, I would sooner blow her up with all the " precious freighting souls" within her, than see such a consummation. When my wonderment had a little subsided, it occurred to me that she would not, perhaps, be so available a battle ship as one of a smaller size : it must be impossible to manœuvre her with any promptitude.　　　*

　*　　　*　　　*　　　*　　　*

My father and —— indulged in sundry right English bits of bragging, as they stood at her stern, looking down the enormous deck. I wish I knew her exact measurements : she is the largest ship ever built, larger than any East Indiaman ; the largest ship in the world. How the sea will groan under her ; nathless in a storm I would rather be in the veriest nutshell that ever was flung from wave-top to wave-top. How she would sink ! she would go down like another Atlantis, poor ship ! I have an amazing horror of drowning. Came home just in time to dine. After dinner, wrote letters ; at six, went to the theatre ; play, Hunchback ; played so-so : the audience are detestable. The majority are so silent that they not only do not applaud the acting, but most religiously forbear to notice all noises in the house, in consequence of which some impudent women amused themselves with talking during the whole play, much " louder than the players." At one time their impertinent racket so bewildered me, that I was all but out, and this without the audience once interfering to silence them ; perhaps, however, that would have been an unwarrantable interference with the sacred liberties of the people. I indulged them with a very significant glance; and at one moment was most strongly tempted to request them to hold their tongues.

Saturday, 27th.

The poor sick lady, whose pretty children I met running about the stairs, sent to say she should be very glad if I would go in and see her: I had had sundry inward promptings to this effect before, but was withheld by the real English dread of intruding. At eleven, went to rehearsal: on my return, called on Mrs. ——.　　　*

　*　　*　　*　　*　　*

　*　　*　　*　　*　　*

She interested me most extremely : I would have stayed long with her, but feared she might exhaust herself by the exertion of conversing. On my return to my own room, I sent her Mr. ——'s annuals, and the volume of Mrs. Hemans's poetry he lent me. Began practising, when in walked that interesting youth, Mr. ——, with a nosegay, as big as himself, in his hand. Flowers, — sweet blooming, fresh, delicious flowers,—in the last days of October; the very sackcloth season of the year. How they do rejoice my spirit. He sat some time, making most excessively fine speeches to me: while he was here, arrived another bouquet from my unknown friend; how nice, to be sure! all but not knowing who they come from. When my visiter was gone, wrote to —— till dinner-time. After dinner, spent nearly the whole afternoon in dressing my pretty flowers. Sent some of them in to Mrs. ——. I don't know why, but it seemed a sad present to make to her; for I almost fear she will never see the blossoms of another year. Yet why do I say that?—is not heaven brighter than even this flowery earth?

    *   *   *   *   *

    *   *   *   *   *

Finished my letter to ——; went to the theatre. My benefit: the Provoked Husband. The house was very good. I played so-so, and looked very nice. What fine breeding this play is, to be sure: it is quite refreshing to act it; but it must be heathen Greek to the American *exclusives*, I should think.

Sunday, 28th.

Had only time to swallow a mouthful of breakfast, and off to church. I must say it requires a deal of fortitude to go into an American church: there are no pew openers, and the people appear to rush indifferently into any seats that are vacant. We went into a pew where there were two women and a man, who did not take up one half of it; but who, nevertheless, looked most ungracious at our coming into it. They did not move to make way or accommodate us, but remained, with very discourteous, unchristian-like sulkiness, spread over twice as much space as they required. The spirit of independence seems to preside paramount, even in the house of God. This congregation, by frequenting an Episcopalian temple, evidently professed the form of faith of the English church; yet they neither uttered the responses, nor observed any one of the directions in the Common Prayer-book. Thus, during portions of the worship where kneeling is enjoined, they sat or stood; and while the Creed was being read, half the auditors were reclining comfortably in their pews: the same thing with the Psalms, and all parts of the service. I suppose their love of freedom will not

suffer them to be amenable to forms, or wear the
exterior of humbleness and homage, even in the
house of the Most High God.*   The whole appearance of the congregation was that of indif-
ference, indolence, and irreverence, and was highly
displeasing to my eye.   After church, came home,

---

* Throughout all the northern states, and particularly
those of New England, the Unitarian form of faith prevails
very extensively.   It appears to me admirably suited to the
spiritual necessities of this portion of the Americans.   They
are a reasoning, not an imaginative, race ; moreover, they are
a hard-working, not an idle, one.   It therefore suits their
necessities, as well as their character, to have a religious
creed divested at once of mysteries at which the rational
mind excepts ; and of long and laborious ceremonies, which
too often engross the time without the attention of the wor-
shipper.   They are poor, too, comparatively speaking ; and
were they so inclined, could little afford, either the splendid
pageantry which the Romish priesthood require, or the less
glaring, but not less expensive revenues which the Episcopalian clergy enjoy.   Their form of religion is a simple one,
a short one, and a cheap one.   Without attempting to dis-
cuss its excellence in the abstract, it certainly appears to me
to be as much fitted for this people, as the marvellous legends and magnificent shows of the Romish church were to
the early European nations.   The church in America is not,
as with us, made a mere means of living : there are no rich
benefices, or over-swelled bishoprics, to be hoped for, by the
man who devotes himself to the service of God's altar : the
pecuniary remuneration of the clergy depends upon the
generosity of their congregations ; and, for the most part, a
sincere love of his vocation must be the American minister's
reward, as it was his original instigation to the work.

and began writing to ——. —— called. He sat some time mending pens for me; and at half-past one D——, he, and I packed ourselves into a coach, and proceeded on to Fair Mount, where we got out, and left the coach to wait for us. The day was bright and bitter cold: the keen spirit-like wind came careering over the crisping waters of the broad river, and carried across the cloudless blue sky the golden showers from the shivering woods. They had not lost their beauty yet; though some of their crimson robes were turned to palest yellow, and through the thin foliage, the dark boughs, and rugged barks showed distinctly, yet the sun shone joyfully on them, and they looked beautiful still; and so did the water, curled into a thousand mimic billows, that came breaking their crystal heads along the curving shore, which, with its shady indentings and bright granite promontories, seemed to lock the river in, and gave it the appearance of a lovely lake. We took the tow-path, by D——'s desire; but found (alas, that it is ever so!) that it was distance lent enchantment to the view. For, though it was very pretty, it had lost some of the beauty it seemed to wear, when we looked down upon it from the woody heights that skirt the road.

On we went, —— and I moderating our strides

to keep pace with D——; and she, puffing, panting, and struggling on to keep pace with us; yet
I was perished, and she was half melted: like all
compromises, it was but a botched business. The
wind was deliciously fresh; and I think, as we
buffeted along in its very face, we should have
made an admirable subject for Bunbury. I, with
my bonnet off, my combs out, and all my hair
flying about, hooked up to ——, who, willow-
like, bent over me, to facilitate my reaching his
arm. D—— following in the rear, her cap and
hair half over her face, her shawl and clothes
fluttering in the blast, her cheeks the colour of
crimson, which, relieved by her green bonnet,
whose sides she grappled tightly down to balk
the wind, had much the effect of a fine carnation
bursting its verdant sheath. I never saw any
thing half so absurd in my life, as we all looked.
Yet it was very pleasant and wholesome, good for
soul and body. After walking for some time, I
asked D—— the hour. It was three, and we
were to dine at four, in order to accommodate the
servants, who, in this land of liberty, make complete slaves of their masters. Horror took possession of us, — how were we ever to get back in
time? To turn back was hopeless: the endless
curvings of the shore, however much we had

admired their graceful sinuosities before, would now have appeared abominable to our straight-forward designs of home, so we agreed to climb the hill and take the upper road — and what a hill it was ! — the sun poured his intense rays down upon it ; and, what with the heat and the wind, and the steep path-way, I thought poor D—— would have died. We turned once as we reached the summit, and I never saw any thing more lovely than the scene we were leaving behind us. The beautiful blue water winding far away between its woody shores ; close below the hill, a small reed-crowned island lying like a gem on the bright river, and a little beyond, the unfinished arches of a white bridge : the opposite shores were bathed with the evening light, and far away the varied colours of the autumnal woods were tinged with the golden glory of sunset. But we were pursued by the thought of four o'clock, and paused but a moment. On we struggled, and at last my frozen blood began to warm ; and by the time we reached the carriage, I was in a fine glow. Certainly exercise is, in itself, very de-lightful, but in scenes like these it is doubly so : the spirit is roused to activity by the natural beauties around, and the fancy and feelings seem to acquire vigour from the quick circulation of the blood, and the muscular energy of the limbs; it is highly excellent.*   We jumped into the coach, adjured the man by all the saints in the calendar

* Whatever progress phrenology may have made in the convictions of people in general, it is much to be hoped, that the physiological principles to which, in the developement of their system, its professors constantly advert, may find favour even with those who are not prepared to admit the truth of the new philosophy of the human intellect.   While we have bodies as well as souls, we must take care of the health of our bodies, if we wish our souls to be healthy.   I have heard many people mention the intimate union of spirit and matter, displayed in the existence of a human being, as highly degrading to the former; however that may be, it is certain that we by no means show our value for the one, by neglecting and maltreating the other; and that if instead of lamenting over the unworthiness of the soul's fleshy partner, we were to improve and correct, and endeavour to ennoble it, we should do the wiser thing.   Upon a well-regulated digestion and circulation, and a healthful nervous system, many of our virtues depend, much of our happiness; and it is almost as impossible to possess a healthy and vigorous mind in a diseased and debilitated body, as it is unusual to see a strong and healthful body allied to an intemperate and ill-governed spirit.   We have some value for the casket which contains our jewel : then should we not have some for that casket to which the jewel absolutely adheres, and which cannot suffer injury itself without communicating it to that which it contains ? Exercise, regularity, and moderation in diet and sleep, well proportioned and varied studies and recreations, — these are none of them subjects of trivial importance to the wise.   Much of our ease and contentedness depends upon them; much of our well-being, much of our *well-doing.*

to put wings to his chariot wheels, and sat con-
cocting plausible lies, by way of excuses, all the
way home. At last we hit upon an admirable
invention. The cause of our being so late was to
be, that we stopped to render our assistance in
reviving an unfortunate young woman, (a lovely
creature, of course,) who had thrown herself into
the Schuylkill, in consequence of some love disappointment, and who was withdrawn just in time
to be preserved. —— was to tell this story with
the gravest face he could summon for the occasion, while we went up to dress, and when we
came down we were to corroborate his statement
as correctly as good chance might enable us. We
dressed in half a minute, and found Mr. ——
sitting with my father, and —— looking amazingly
demure. It seemed, however, that no remark
had been made, nor question asked, about our
protracted perambulations, so that we had actually
thrown away all our ingenuity. This vexed me so
much, that in the middle of dinner I introduced the
topic of drowning, and, with a lamentable face,
related the circumstance; but, alas! one of my
auditors was occupied with a *matelotte d'anquilles,*
another with an oyster *vol-au-vent,* and all the
pretty girls in creation might have been drowned,
without the loss in any degree affecting the evi-

dent satisfaction which the above subjects of me-
ditation seemed to afford the gentlemen : what
selfish brutes men are! shocking.   Our invention
was thus twice thrown away : one said " Humph ! "
and the other " Ha ! " and that was the extent of
their sympathy.   After dinner, came up to my
own room, lay down, and fairly slept till coffee
was announced.   Came down with half an eye
open, and found the circle augmented by the
delectable presence of Mr. ——.   What an original that youth is.   They talked politics, abused
republicanism, lauded aristocracy, drank tea, took
snuff, ate cakes, and pottered a deal.   My father
was going fast asleep, —— was making a thousand signs to me to go to the piano, when Mr.
—— rose to depart: the other gentlemen took
the hint, and left us at half-past ten.

Tuesday, 30th.

At eleven o'clock, went to rehearsal : came home,
began letter to ——.   Called with my father upon
Mrs. —— : the servant committed that awfullest
of blunders, letting one into the house, and then
finding out that nobody was at home.*   Came

---

* I think it has not been my good fortune, in more than
six instances, during my residence in this country, to find

home, practised for some time: all of a sudden
the door opened, and in walked Colonel ——
with my father. He had just arrived from New

---

ladies " at home" in the morning. The first reason for this
is, the total impossibility of having a housekeeper; the
American servants steadfastly refusing to obey *two* mistresses;
the being subservient to any appears, indeed, a dreadful
hardship to them. Of course this compels the lady of the
house to enter into all those minute daily details, which with
us devolve upon the superintendent servant, and she is thus
condemned, at least for some part of the morning, to the
store-room or the kitchen. In consequence of this, her toilet
is seldom completed until about to take her morning promenade; and I have been a good deal surprised, more than
once, at being told, when I called, that " the ladies were
dressing, but would be down immediately." This is French;
the disorderly slouching about half the morning in a careless
undress being, unluckily, quite compatible with that exquisite
niceness of appearance with which the Parisian ladies edify
their streets so much, and their homes so little. Another
very disagreeable result of this arrangement is, that when
you are admitted into a house in the morning, the rooms appear as if they never were used : there are no books lying
about, no work-tables covered with evidences of constant
use, and if there is a piano, it is generally closed; the whole
giving one an uninhabited feel that is extremely uncomfortable. As to a morning lounge in a lady's boudoir, or a gentleman's library, the thing's unheard of; to be sure there are
no loungers, where every man is tied to a counting-house
from morning till night; and therefore no occasion for those
very pleasant sanctums devoted to gossiping, political, literary,
and scandalous.

York. He dined with us. After dinner, finished letter to ——. At six, went to the theatre. The house was very good; play, Much Ado about Nothing. I played well; but what an audience it is! I have been often recommended, in cases of nervousness on the stage, to consider the audience as just so many cabbages, and, indeed, a small stretch of fancy would enable me to do so here. Colonel —— supped with us. Found an invitation to dinner from the ——. " One exception makes a rule," say the scholars; by that same token, therefore, the Philadelphians are about the most inhospitable set of people it ever was my good fortune to fall in with.* Towards

* I am sure there is no town in Europe where my father could fix his residence for a week, without being immediately found out by most of the residents of any literary acquirements, or knowledge of matters relating to art; I am sure that neither in France, Italy, or Germany, could he take up his abode in any city, without immediately being sought by those best worth knowing in it. I confess it surprised me, therefore, when I found that, during a month's residence in Philadelphia, scarcely a creature came near us, and but one house was hospitably opened to us; as regards myself, I have no inclination whatever to speak upon the subject; but it gave me something like a feeling of contempt, not only for the charities, but for the good taste of the Philadelphians, when I found them careless and indifferent towards one whose name alone is a passport into every refined and cul-

the end of supper, we fell into a strange discussion as to the nature of existence. A vain and fruitless talk, after all; for life shall be happy or sad, not, indeed, according to its events, but according to the nature of the individuals to whom these events befall. Colonel —— maintained that life was in itself desirable; abounding in blessings, replete with comforts, a fertile land, where still, as one joy decays, another springs up to flourish in its place. He said that he felt thankful every day, and every hour of the day, for his existence; that he feared death, only because life was an absolute enjoyment, and that he would willingly, to-morrow, accept the power of beginning his again, even though he should be placed on the world's threshold, a lonely, friendless beggar: so sure was he that his prospects would brighten, and friends spring up to him, and plenty reward labour, and life become pleasant, ere it had grown many years old. How widely human beings differ! It was but an hour before, that I, in

---

tivated society in Europe. Every where else, in America, our reception was very different; and I can only attribute the want of courtesy we met with in Philadelphia to the greater prevalence of that very small spirit of dignity which is always afraid of committing itself.

counting how many stars I had already seen go down below the horizon of existence—Weber, Lawrence, Scott, all of whom I have known, — was saying to D——, " How sad a thing, and strange, life is ! " adding, what I repent me for, " I wish that I were dead ! " Oh, how can any human being, who looks abroad into the world, and within upon himself, who sees the wondrous mystery of all things, the unabidingness which waits on all matter, the imperfection which clogs all spirit; who notes the sovereignty of change over the inanimate creation, of disease, decay, and death over man's body, of blindness and delusion over his mind, of sin over his soul; who beholds the frailty of good men; who feels the miserable inconsistency of his own nature; the dust and ashes of which our love, and what we love, is made; the evil that, like an unwholesome corpse, still clings to our good; the sorrow that, like its shadow, still walks behind our joy;—oh, who that sees all this can say that this life is other than sad — most sad ? Yet, while I write this, God forbid that I should therefore want eyes to see, or sense to feel, the blessings wherewith he has blessed it; the rewards with which he sweetens our task, the flowers wherewith he cheers our journey's road, the many props wherewith he supports our feet in it. Yet

of all these, the sweetest, the brightest, the
strongest, are those which our soul draws from him,
the end of its desire, not those it finds here. And
how should not that spirit yearn for its accomplishment? If we seek knowledge here, a thousand
mists arise between our incapable senses and the
truth; how, then, should we not wish to cast away
this darkness, and soar to the fountains of all
light? If we strive to employ those faculties
which, being of our soul, have the strength and
enduring of immortality, the objects whereon we
expend them here are vague, evanescent, dis-
appointing; how then should we not desire to
find food for our capacities, abiding as themelves?
If we long to love — ah, are not the creatures in
whom we centre our affections frail, capable of
change; perishable, born to decay? How then
should we not look with unutterable yearning for
that life where affection is unchangeable, eternal?
Surely, if all the hopes, the fears, the aims, the
tendings of our soul, have but their beginning here,
it is most natural, it is most fitting, to turn to that
future where they shall be fulfilled. But there
s a road between.   *   *   *   *
      *   *   *   *   *

A break—a break—a break! So much the better; for the two last days have been nothing but annoyance, hardwork, and heartache.　　*　　*

*　　　*　　　*　　　*　　　*

Friday, November 2d.

A bright sunny day; too hot for a fire; windows open, shutters closed, and the room full of flowers. How the sweet summer-time stays lingering here. Found Colonel —— in the drawing-room. After breakfast, began writing to ——. Mr. —— called: he stayed but a short time, and went out with Colonel ——. My father went out soon after, and I began to practise. Mrs. —— came in and sat with me: she played to me, and sang " Should those fond hopes ever leave thee." Her voice was as thin as her pale transparent hands. She appeared to me much better than when last I saw her; but presently told me she had just been swallowing eighty drops of laudanum, poor thing ! When she was gone, went on practising, and writing, till my father came home. Walked with him and D—— to call on old Lady ——. The day was so hot that I could scarcely endure my boa. The election was going on; the streets full of rabblement, the air full of huzzaing, and the sky obscured with star-spangled banners, and

villanous transparencies of " Old Hickory *,"
hung out in all directions. We went round the
Town House, and looked at the window out of
which Jefferson read the Act of Independence,
that proclaimed the separation between England
and America.† Called at a music-shop, tossed

* The familiar appellation by which the democracy de-
signate their favourite, General Jackson. The hickory
wood is the tallest and the toughest possible, and by no
means a bad type of some of the President's physical and
moral attributes. Hickory poles, as they are called, are
erected before most of the taverns frequented by the
thorough-going Jacksonites; and they are sometimes sur-
mounted by the glorious " Cap of Liberty," that much
abused symbol, which has presided over so many scenes of
political frenzy.

† In beholding this fine young giant of a world, with all
its magnificent capabilities for greatness, I think every Englishman must feel unmingled regret at the unjust and unwise
course of policy which alienated such a child from the
parent government. But, at the same time, it is impossible
to avoid seeing that some other course must, ere long, have
led to the same result, even if England had pursued a more
maternal course of conduct towards America. No one, beholding this enormous country, stretching from ocean to
ocean, watered with ten thousand glorious rivers, combining
every variety of climate and soil, therefore, every variety of
produce and population; possessing within itself every re-
source that other nations are forced either to buy abroad, or
to create substitutes for at home; no one, seeing the in-
ternal wealth of America, the abundant fertility of the
earth's surface, the riches heaped below it, the unparalleled

over heaps of music, bought some, and ordered
some to be sent home for me to look over. Came

---

facilities for the intercourse of men, and the interchange of
their possessions throughout its vast extent, can for an instant indulge the thought that such a country was ever
destined to be an appendage to any other in the world, or
that any chain of circumstances whatever could have long
maintained in dependence a people furnished with every
means of freedom and greatness. But far from regretting
that America has thrown off her allegiance, and regarding her
as a rebellious subject, and irreverent child, England will
surely, ere long, learn to look upon this country as the in-
heritor of her glory; the younger England, destined to per-
petuate the language, the memory, the virtues of the noble
land from which she is descended. Loving and honouring
my country as I do, I cannot look upon America with any
feeling of hostility. I not only hear the voice of England in
the language of this people, but I recognise in all their best
qualities, their industry, their honesty, their sturdy independence of spirit, the very witnesses of their origin — they
are English; no other people in the world would have licked
us as they did; nor any other people in the world built
up, upon the ground they won, so sound, and strong, and
fair an edifice.

With regard to what I have said in the beginning of this
note, of the many reasons which combined to render this
country independent of all others, I think they in some
measure tell against the probability of its long remaining at
unity with itself. Such numerous and clashing interests;
such strong and opposite individuality of character between
the northern and southern states; above all, such enormous
extent of country; seem rationally to present many points

home, put out things for the theatre. Dined at
three.   *   *   *   *   *

   *   *   *   *   *

   *   *   *   *   *

Received another beautiful nosegay. After dinner, went on with letter to ——; tried over my
music; Heber's song that I wanted is not among
them. At six, went to the theatre. The sunset
was glorious, the uprising of the moon most
beautiful. There is an intensity, an earnestness
about the colour of the sky, and the light of its
bright inhabitants here, that is lovely and solemn,
beyond any thing I ever saw. Can Italy have
brighter heavens than these? surely, nothing can
exceed the beauty of these days and nights. We
were obliged to go all manner of roundabouts to
the play-house, in order to avoid the rabble that
choked up the principal streets. I, by way of
striking salutary awe into the hearts of all rioters
who might come across our path, brandished my
father's sword out of the coach window the whole
way along. The play was Venice Preserved; my
father played Jaffier.   *   *   *

   *   *   *   *   *

---

of insecurity; many probabilities of separations and break-
ingsasunder; but all this lies far on, and I leave it to those
who have good eyes for a distance.

I played pretty well.   The house was very good;
but at the end I really was half dead.   *

*   *   *   *   *

*   *   *   *   *

On our return home, met a procession of
electioneerers carrying triangular paper lanterns
upon poles, with " sentiments" political scribbled
thereon, which, however, I could not distinguish.
Found a most exquisite nosegay waiting for me
at home, so sweet, so brilliant, so fragrant, and
fresh. *   *   *   *   *

*   *   *   *   *

Found nothing for supper that I could fancy.
Drank some tea, wrote journal.   Colonel ——
came in after supper, and wondered that I had
played better to my father's Jaffier, than to Mr.
Keppel's.   Heaven bless the world, for a *con-
glomerated amalgamation* of fools !

Monday, 5th.

Guy Fawlk's day, and no squibs, no firing of
pistols, n o bonfires, nor parading about of fero-
cious looking straw men. Ah ! these poor people
never had a king and two houses of parliament,
and don't know what a mercy it is they weren't
blown up before they passed the reform bill.

Now if such an accident should occur to them, they'd all be sure to be blown straight into heaven, and hang there. Rose at half-past five. Oh, I quite agree with the Scotch song,

> " Up in the morning's na for me,
> Up in the morning early;
> I'd rather watch a winter's night,
> Than rise in the morning early."

Dressed myself by candle light. Mrs. —— sent in to ask me if I would see her, but I had not time. Sent her a note, and received, in exchange, the seed of what I suspect is the wood laurel, common in this country, but unknown in ours. Started from the Mansion House (which is a very nice inn, kept by the civilest of people,) at six, and reached the quay just in time to meet the first rosy breaking of the clouds over the Delaware. *   *   *
  *   *   *   *   *
  *   *   *   *   *

I am sorry to leave Philadelphia. I like the town, and the little I have seen of its inhabitants, very much; I mean in private, for they are intolerable audiences. There is an air of stability, of well to do, and occasionally of age, in the town, that reminds me of England. Then, as far as my yesterday's dinner will allow me to judge, I should say, that not only the style of living, but the society was superior to that which I saw in New York. Certainly, both the entertainment itself, and the guests, were irreproachable; the first was in very good taste, the latter appeared to me well-informed, and very agreeable. The morning, in spite of all ——'s persuasive prophecies, was beautiful beyond description. The river like the smoothest glass. The sky was bright and cloudless, and along the shores, the distinctness with which each smallest variation of form, or shade of colour, was reflected in the clear mirror of the Delaware, was singularly beautiful and fairy-like. The tints of the woods were what no words can convey the slightest idea of. Now, a whole track of withered oaks, of a red brick hue, like a forest scorched with fire; now, a fresh thicket of cedars, of the brightest green; then, wide screens of mingled trees, where the foliage was one gorgeous mixture of vermilion, dark maroon, tender green, golden yellow, and deep geranium. The whole land at a distance appearing to lie under an atmosphere of glowing colour, richer than any crimson mantle that ever clothed the emperors of the olden world; all this, illuminated by a sun, which we should have thought too hot for June. It was very beautiful. I did not, however, see much of it, for I was overcome with fatigue, and slept, both in the steam-boat, and in the stage-coach. When we embarked on the Raritan, I had intended lying down in the cabin, and taking my sleep fairly out, but the jolting of those bitter roads had made every one of the women sick, and the cabin was horrible beyond expression. Came up on deck, and worked till within a quarter of a mile of New York, when I went on the upper deck, and walked about with Colonel ———. I asked Captain Seymour how often the engine would strike in a minute; he told me, thirty-six times. By the by, we had a race coming down the Raritan, with the Union steam-boat. The Water Witch beat her hollow; but she came so near as to make our water rough, and so impede our progress, that I thought we should have had a concussion; there is something very exciting in emulation, certainly. The sun went down in a watery, gloomy sky, though the day had been so fine; and when we got sight of the Narrows, sky, and sea, and land, were all of a dark leaden hue. Our second landing at New York was rather melancholy: shall I ever forget the first? Came up to our comfortless quarters at the American; dressed, and dined, and began finishing my letter to dear ——, when they brought me in another from her, by the packet that has just come in.   *   *   *

    *   *   *   *   *

    *   *   ~   *   *

Tuesday, 6th.

It poured with rain. Lucky we did not follow ——'s advice, else we should have been miserably progressing through rain and wretchedness, or perhaps sticking fast in the mud. Went and took a warm bath; came home, breakfasted; after breakfast, practised for an hour; finished letter to ——; wrote to my mother; dined at five. After dinner, Colonel —— called, and very nearly caused a blow up between me and my father: he came preaching to me the necessity of restoring those lines of Bianca's, in the judgment scene, which were originally omitted, afterwards restored by me at Milman's request, and again cut out, on finding that they only lengthened the scene, without producing the slightest effect. My father appeared perfectly to agree with me, but added, that I might as well oblige the people. I straightforth said I would do no such thing.

People sitting before the curtain must not come and tell me what I am to do behind it. Not one out of a hundred, in the first place, understand what they are talking about; and why, therefore, am I to alter my work at their suggestion, when each particular scene has cost me more consideration than they ever bestowed upon any whole play in all their lives. Besides, it would be with me and my parts, as with the old man, his son, and his ass, in the fable of old; I should never have done altering, and yet never satisfy any body, for the most universal talent I know of, is that of finding fault. So, all things well considered, the New Yorkians must e'en be contented with the judgment of Miss O'Neill, my father, and their obedient, humble servant. Worked till tea-time; after tea, wrote letters till now, bed-time.

Wednesday, 7th.

Our breakfast was so bad, none of us could eat any thing. After breakfast, despatched letters to Mr. ———, for England. Practised for an hour, — sketched for an hour. 　　*　　　　*

　　*　　　*　　　*　　　*　　　*

　　*　　　*　　　*　　　*　　　*

M 3

At half-past one, went out with my father to walk on the Battery, while Colonel —— and D—— went to ——, to see if we could get decent lodgings, and wholesome eatables there. The day was melancholy, grey, cold; with a full, fresh wind, whirling the rattling leaves along, and rippling the leaden waters of the wide estuary that opens before this beautiful parade. The Jersey shore and Staten Island, with their withered woods all clothed in their dark, warm, autumnal hues, at a distance reminded me of the heathery hills of Scotland; they had that dark purple richness of colouring.

* * * * *

* * * * *

D—— and Colonel —— joined us, and we walked up Broadway together : my father left me to go with them, and look at our proposed dwelling. It is all in vain struggling with one's fate ; 't is clear they haven't the most distant idea of the comforts of life in these parts. Darkness, dinginess, and narrowness, were the attributes of the apartments into which we were shown; then, as the Colonel had never eaten in the house, he did not know what our food might be — pleasant this ! *Resolved,* that we were better off where we are, and so returned to the American. Sketched and practised for some time longer. Mr. —— called to go with my father to Mrs. ——'s, where they were to dine. He certainly is one of the handsomest men I ever saw; but he looks half dead, and is working himself to death, it should seem.   *   *

    *   *   *   *   *

    *   *   *   *   *

He told me that Boston was the most charming town in America.   *   *   *

    *   *   *   *   *

Put away things, while D—— unpacked them. Dressed for dinner. Dined at five; afterwards proceeded in the unpacking and stowing away.

    *   *   *   *   *

I was interrupted by the announcement of an incomprehensible cognomen, which solved itself in the shape of Mr. ——, who walked in, sat down, and began talking a deal of nonsense. I worked, that I might not go to sleep. He was most exceedingly odd and dauldrummish. I think he was a little " how com'd you so indeed." He sat very near me, spoke exceedingly drowsily, and talked an amazing quantity of thickish philosophy, and moral and sentimental potter. I bore it as well as I could, till ten o'clock, when I asked him how long it was " reckoned " discreet, in this country, to prolong evening visits; whereupon he arose and took his departure.   *   *

*   *   *   *   *

*   *   *   *   *

Worked at the ornaments of my Bianca dress, finished one, and wrote journal.

Thursday, 8th.

*   *   *   *   *

After breakfast, worked at my dress till late; Mr. —— called. Put away goods and chattels; put out things for the theatre. A brother of Mr. —— called upon us, and sat some time : when he was gone, came back to my room to finish the ornaments for my dress. This day has been spent in the thorough surroundings of my vocation; foil stone, glass beads, and brass tape ! —— came just before dinner; and at the end of it, Colonel —— called. He read us a paragraph in one of the Philadelphia papers, upon me, and all my good parts; there was actually a column of them. It was well written, for I was absolute perfection; excepting, indeed, in one respect, the hauteur and disdain with which I had treated the " *rank* and fashion of Philadelphia." Now this was not true, for, to speak candidly, I did not know that there were such things as rank and fashion in all America. However, the article made me laugh extremely, for, as I could not help observing, " there are *real* lords and ladies in my country." †

* * * * *

† I think the pretension to pre-eminence, in the various societies of North America, is founded on these grounds. In Boston, a greater degree of mental cultivation; in New York, the possession of wealth; and a lady, of whom I enquired the other day what constituted the superiority of the *aristocracy* in Philadelphia, replied, — " Why, birth, to be sure." Virginia and Carolina, indeed, long prided themselves upon their old family names, which were once backed by large possessions; and for many years the southern gentlemen might not improperly be termed the aristocracy of America; but the estates of those who embraced the king's cause during the rebellion were confiscated; and the annulling the laws of entail and primogeniture, and the parcelling out of property under the republican form of government, have gradually destroyed the fortunes of most of the old southern families. Still, they hold fast to the spirit of their former superiority, and from this circumstance, and the possession of slaves, which exempts them from the drudgery of earning their livelihood, they are a much less mercantile race of men than those of the northern states; generally better informed, and infinitely more polished in their manners. The few southerners with whom I have become acquainted resemble Europeans both in their accomplishments, and the quiet and reserve of their manners. On my remarking, one day, to a Philadelphia gentleman, whose general cultivation keeps pace with his political and financial talents, how singular the contrast was between the levelling spirit of this government, and the separating and dividing spirit of American society, he replied, that if his many vocations allowed him time, he should like to write a novel illustrating the curious struggle which exists throughout this country between its political

Came to my own room, — refurbished my green
velvet bonnet. 'T is a worthy old thing that, and
looks amazingly well. The cold weather is setting
in very bitterly to-day ; we were obliged to have a
fire. Heard my father his part : whilst saying it,
he received a subpœna on some business between
Mr. —— and Mr. ——. At a quarter to six,
went to the theatre. Play, Fazio; house very fine;
dress like a bonfire. I played well, but then my
father was the Fazio. The people cried abundantly. Mrs. —— was shocked at having to play
that naughty woman Aldabella (I wish they would
let me try that part); and when the Duke dismissed
her in the last scene, picked up her train, and
flounced off in a way that made the audience for
to laugh. Coming home, Mr. —— overtook us.
My father asked him in, but he excused himself;
before, however, we were well seated, he had re-
pented the refusal, and came rushing back.
Colonel —— came in, and they both of them
supped with us, discussing many matters of pith.

---

and its social institutions. The anomaly is, indeed, striking.
Democracy governs the land; whilst, throughout society, a
contrary tendency shows itself, wherever it can obtain the
very smallest opportunity. It is unfortunate for America,
that its aristocracy must, of necessity, be always one of
wealth.

Received a nosegay, as big as myself, of dahlias and other autumnal flowers.　　*　　　　*

　　*　　　　*　　　　*　　　　*　　　　*

The moon is resplendent! the earth is flooded with her cold light — beautiful!　By the by, *last night*, at three o'clock this morning, I was awakened by music.　It was a military band playing Yankee Doodle, the national anthem of the Americans, accompanied by the tramp of a considerable body of men.　They took the direction of the Park, and there halted, when I heard a single voice haranguing for a length of time, with occasional interruptions of vehement huzzas, and rolling of drums.　And anon, the march struck up again, grew faint, and died into the stillness of night.　　*　　　　*　　　　*　　　　*

　　*　　　　*　　　　*　　　　*　　　　*

I was much bounden to the Jacksonites, who are carrying it by fair means or foul.　One man, I was assured, voted nine times over!　He was an Irishman, and it is to be presumed, a tailor.

Saturday, 10*th.*

Skipped yesterday: so much the better, for though it began, like May, with flowers and sunshine, it ended, like December, with the sulks, and a fit of crying. The former were furnished me by my friends and Heaven, the latter, by myself and the devil.   *   *   *

   *   *   *   *   *

   *   *   *   *   *

At six o'clock, D—— roused me; and grumpily enough I arose. I dressed myself by candlelight in a hurry. Really, by way of a party of pleasure, 't is too abominable to get up in the middle of the night this fashion. At half-past six, Colonel —— came; and as soon as I could persuade myself into my clothes, we set off to walk to the quay. Just as we were nearing the bottom of Barclay Street, the bell rang from the steam-boat, to summon all loiterers on board; and forthwith we rushed, because in this country steam and paddles, like wind and tide in others, wait for no man. We got on board in plenty time, but D—— was nearly killed with the pace at which we had walked, in order to do so. One of the first persons we saw was Mr. ——, who was going up to his father's place beyond West Point, by name Hyde Park, which sounds mighty magnificent. I did not remain long on the second deck, but ascended to the first with Colonel ——, and paced to and fro with infinite zeal till breakfast-time. The morning was grey and sad looking, and I feared we should not have a fine day: however, towards eight o'clock the grey clouds parted, and the blue, serene eyes of heaven looked down upon the waters; the waves began to sparkle, though the sun had not yet appeared; the sky was lighter, and faint shadows began to appear beside the various objects that surrounded us, all which symptoms raised our hopes of the weather. At eight o'clock, we went down to breakfast. Nobody who has not seen it, can conceive the strange aspect of the long room of one of these fine boats at meal-time. The crowd, the hurry, the confusion of tongues, like the sound of many waters, the enormous consumption of eatables, the mingled demands for more, the cloud of black waiters hovering down the sides of the immense tables, the hungry, eager faces seated at them, form altogether a most amusing subject of contemplation, and a caricaturist would find ample matter for his vein in almost every other devouring countenance. As far as regards the speed, safety, and convenience with which these vessels enable one to perform what would be in any other conveyance most fatiguing journeys, they are admirable inventions. The way in which they are conducted, too, deserves the highest commendation. Nothing can exceed the comfort with which they are fitted up, the skill with which they are managed, and the order and alacrity with which passengers are taken up from, or landed at, the various points along the river. The steamer goes at the rate of fifteen miles an hour ; and in less than two minutes, when approaching any place of landing, the engine stops, the boat is lowered — the captain always convoys his passengers himself from the steamer to the shore — away darts the tiny skiff, held by a rope to the main boat; as soon as it grazes the land, its freight, animate and inanimate, is bundled out, the boat hauls itself back in an instant, and immediately the machine is in motion, and the vessel again bounding over the water like a race-horse. * Doubtless all this has many and great advantages; but to an English person, the mere cir-

* Of course the captain is undisputed master of the boat, and any disorders, quarrels, &c., which may arise, are settled by his authority. Any passenger, guilty of misbehaviour, is either confined or sent immediately on shore, no matter how far from his intended destination. I once saw very summary justice performed on a troublesome fellow who was disturbing the whole society on board one of the North River steamers. He was put into the small boat with the captain and a stout looking sailor, and very comfortably deposited on some rafts which were floating along shore, about twenty miles below West Point, whither he was bound.

cumstance of being the whole day in a crowd is a nuisance. As to privacy at any time, or under any circumstances, 't is a thing that enters not into the imagination of an American. They do not seem to comprehend that to be from sunrise to sunset one of a hundred and fifty people confined in a steam-boat is in itself a great misery, or that to be left by one's self and to one's self can ever be desirable. They live all the days of their lives in a throng, eat at ordinaries of two or three hundred, sleep five or six in a room, take pleasure in droves, and travel by swarms. †   *

*   *   *   *   *

In spite, therefore, of all its advantages, this mode of journeying has its drawbacks. And the greatest of all, to me, is the being *companioned* by so many strangers, who crowd about you, pursue their conversation in your very ears, or, if they like it better, listen to yours, stare you out of all countenance, and squeeze you out of all comfort. It is perfectly intolerable to me; but then I have

---

† The quantity of one's companions in these conveyances is not more objectionable than their quality sometimes. As they are the only vehicles, and the fares charged are extremely low, it follows, necessarily, that all classes and sorts of people congregate in them, from the ragged Irish emigrant and the boorish back-countryman, to the gentleman of the senate, the supreme court, and the president himself.

more than even the national English abhorrence of coming in contact with strangers. There is no moment of my life when I would not rather be alone, than in company; and feeling, as I often do, the society of even those I love a burden, the being eternally surrounded by indifferent persons is a positive suffering that interferes with every enjoyment, and makes pleasure three parts endurance. I think this constant living in public is one reason why the young women here are much less retiring and shy than English girls. Instead of the domestic privacy in which women among us are accustomed to live, and move, and have their being, here they are incessantly, as Mr. —— says, " *en evidence.*" Accustomed to the society of strangers, mixing familiarly with persons of whom they know nothing earthly, subject to the gaze of a crowd from morning till night, pushing, and pressing, and struggling in self-defence, conversing, and being conversed with, by the chance companions of a boarding-house, a steam-boat, or the hotel of a fashionable watering-place, they must necessarily lose every thing like reserve or bashfulness of deportment, and become free and familiar in their manners, and noisy and unrefined in their tone and style of conversation.* An

* The manners of the young girls of America appear singularly free to foreigners; and until they become better

English girl of sixteen, put on board one of these
Noah's arks (for verily there be clean and unclean

---

acquainted with the causes which produce so unrestrained a
deportment, they are liable to take disadvantageous and mistaken impressions with regard to them. The term which I
should say applied best to the tone and carriage of American
girls from ten to eighteen, is hoydenish; laughing, giggling,
romping, flirting, screaming at the top of their voices, running
in and out of shops, and spending a very considerable portion
of their time in lounging about in the streets. In Philadelphia and Boston, almost all the young ladies attend classes
or day schools; and in the latter place I never went out,
morning, noon, or evening, that I did not meet, in some of
the streets round the Tremont House, a whole bevy of young
school girls, who were my very particular friends, but who,
under pretext of going to, or returning from, school, appeared
to me to be always laughing, and talking, and running about
in the public thoroughfares; a system of education which we
should think by no means desirable. The entire liberty which
the majority of young ladies are allowed to assume, at an age
when in England they would be under strict nursery discipline, appears very extraordinary; they not only walk alone
in the streets, but go out into society, where they take a
determined and leading part, without either mother, aunt, or
chaperon of any sort; custom, which renders such an appendage necessary with us, entirely dispenses with it here;
and though the reason of this is obvious enough in the narrow circles of these small towns, where every body knows
every body, the manners of the young ladies do not derive
any additional charm from the perfect self-possession which
they thus acquire. Shiness appears to me to be a quality
utterly unknown to either man, woman, or child in America.
The girls, from the reasons above stated; and the boys, from

beasts in them), would feel and look like a scared
thing.   To return to our progress.   After losing

---

being absolutely thrown into the world, and made men of
business before they are sixteen, are alike deficient in any
thing like diffidence; and I really have been all but discon-
certed at the perfect assurance with which I have been
addressed, upon any and every subject, by little men and
women just half way through their teens. That very common
character amongst us, a shy man, is not to be met with in
these latitudes.   An American conversing on board one of
their steam-boats is immediately surrounded, particularly if
his conversation, though strictly directed to one individual,
is of a political nature; in an instant a ring of spectators is
formed round him, and whereas an Englishman would become silent at the very first appearance of a listener, an
American, far from seeming abashed at this "audience," continues his discourse, which thus assumes the nature of an
harangue, with perfect equanimity, and feels no annoyance
whatever at having unfolded his private opinions of men and
matters to a circle of forty or fifty people whom they could
in no possible way concern. Speechifying is a very favourite
species of exhibition with the men here, by the by; and, besides being self-possessed, they are all remarkably fluent.
Really eloquent men are just as rare in this country as in any
other, but the " gift of the gab " appears to me more widely
disseminated amongst Americans than any other people in the
world.   Many things go to make good speakers of them:
great acuteness, and sound common sense, sufficient general
knowledge, and great knowledge of the world, an intense
interest in every political measure, no matter how trivial in
itself, no sense of bashfulness, and a great readiness of expression.   But to return to the manners of the young American girls : — It is Rousseau, I think, who says, " Dans un

sight of New York, the river becomes narrower in its bed, and the banks on either side assume a higher and more rocky appearance. A fine range of basaltic rock, called the Palisadoes, rising to a height of some hundred feet (I guess), immediately from the water on the left, forms a natural rampart, overhanging the river for several miles. The colour of the basalt was greenish grey, and con-

---

pays ou les mœurs sont pures, les filles seront faciles, et les femmes severes." This applies particularly well to the carriage of the American women. When remarking to a gentleman once the difference between the manners of my own young countrywomen and his, I expressed my disapprobation of the education which led to such a result, he replied, " You forget the comparatively pure state of morals in our country, which admits of this degree of freedom in our young women, without its rendering them liable to insult or misconstruction." This is true, and it is also most true, for I have seen repeated instances of it, that those very girls, whose manners have been most displeasing to my European ways of feeling, whom I should have pointed out as romps and flirts pre-eminent, not only make excellent wives, but from the very moment of their marriage seem to forsake society, and devote themselves exclusively to household duties and retirement. But that I have seen and known of repeated instances of this, I could scarcely have believed it, but it is the case; and a young American lady, speaking upon this subject, said to me, " We enjoy ourselves before marriage; but in your country, girls marry to obtain a greater degree of freedom, and indulge in the pleasures and dissipations of society." She was not, I think, greatly mistaken.

trasted finely with the opposite shore, whose softer
undulations were yet clothed with verdure, and
adorned with patches of woodland, robed in the
glorious colours of an American autumn. While
despatching breakfast, the reflection of the sun's
rays on the water flickered to and fro upon the
cabin ceiling; and through the loop-hole windows
we saw the bright foam round the paddles sparkling
like frothed gold in the morning light. On our
return to the deck, the face of the world had
become resplendent with the glorious sunshine that
now poured from the east; and rock and river,
earth and sky, shone in intense and dazzling
brilliancy. The broad Hudson curled into a
thousand crisp billows under the fresh north-wester
that blew over it. The vaporous exhalations of
night had melted from the horizon, and the bold,
rocky range of one shore, and exquisite rolling
outline of the other, stood out in fair relief against
the deep serene of the blue heavens.   *

    *   *   *   *   *

    *   *   *   *   *

I remained on deck without my bonnet, walking
to and fro, and enjoying the delicious wind that
was as bracing as a shower-bath. Mr. —— most
civilly offered me, when I returned to New York,
the use of a horse, and himself as escort to a beau-

tiful ride beyond Hoboken, which proffer was very gratefully received by me. Colonel —— introduced me to an old man of the name of ——.

* * * * *

* * * * *

A jester, and a long story-teller; — a man whom it would be awful to meet when you were too late for dinner, still more awful on your progress to a rendezvous; — a man to whom a listener is a God-send, and a button an anchor of discoursing for half a day. He made me laugh once or twice heartily. As we passed the various points of the river, to which any interest, legendary or historical, attached, each of my three companions drew my attention to it; and I had, pretty generally, three variations of the same anecdote at each point of observation. On we boiled past Spitendevil creek*, where the waters of the broad Hudson join those of the East River, and circle with their silver arms the island of Manhattan. Past the last stupendous reach of the Palisadoes, which, stretching out into an endless promontory, seems to grow with the mariner's onward progress, and bears witness to the justice with which Hudson, on his exploring voyage up the river, christened it, the " weary

* For the origin of this curious name, see that interesting and veracious work, the history of Knickerbocker.

point." Past the thick masses of wood that mark
the shadowy site of Sleepy Hollow.* Past the
marble prison of Sing Sing; and Tarrytown, where
poor Andrè was taken; and on the opposite shore,
saw the glimmering white buildings, among which
his tomb reposes. — By the by, for a bit of the
marvellous, which I dearly love. I am credibly
informed, that on the day the traitor Arnold died,
in England, a thunderbolt struck the tree that grew
above Andrè's tomb here, on the shores of the
Hudson — nice, that! Crossed the broad, glorious,
Tappan Sea, where the shores receding, form a
huge basin, where the brimming waters roll in an
expanse of lake-like width, yet hold their rapid
current to the ocean, themselves a running sea.
The giant shadows of the mountains on the left,
falling on the deep basin at their feet, the triumphant sunlight that made the restless mirror that
reflected it too bright for the eye to rest upon, the
sunny shores to the right, rising and falling in every
exquisite form that hill and dale can wear, the
jutting masses of granite, glittering like the diamond
rocks of fairy-land, in the sun, the golden waves
flinging themselves up every tiny crevice, the glowing crimson foliage of the distant woods, the fresh

* Famous as the scene of Ichabod Crane's exploits.

vivid green of the cedars, that rifted their strong roots in every stony cleft, and threw a semblance of summer over these November days — all, all was beautiful, and full of brightness. We passed the lighthouse of Stony Point, now the peaceful occupant of the territory, where the blood in English veins was poured out by English hands, during the struggle between old established tyranny and the infant liberties of this giant world. Over all and each, the blessed sky bent its blue arch, resplendently clear and bright, while far away the distant summits of the Highlands rose one above another, shutting in the world, and almost appearing as though each bend of the river must find us locked in their shadowy circle, without means of onward progress.   *   *   *

*   *   *   *   *

*   *   *   *   *

At every moment, the scene varied ; at every moment, new beauty and grandeur was revealed to us ; at every moment, the delicious lights and shadows fell with richer depth and brightness upon higher openings into the mountains, and fairer bends of the glorious river. At about a quarter to eleven, the buildings of West Point were seen, perched upon the rock side, overhanging the water; above, the woody rise, upon whose summit stands the large hotel, the favourite resort of visiters during the summer season; rising again above this, the ruins of Fort Putnam, poor André's prison-house, overlooking the Hudson and its shores; and towering high beyond them all, the giant hills, upon whose brown shoulders the trees looked like bristles standing up against the sky. We left the boat, or rather she left us, and presently we saw her holding her course far up the bright water, and between the hills; where, framed by the dark mountains with the sapphire stream below and the sapphire sky above, lay the bright little town of Newburgh, with its white buildings glittering in the sunshine.   *   *   *   *

*   *   *   *   *

*   *   *   *   *

We toiled up the ascent, which, though by comparison with its overpeering fellows inconsiderable, was a sufficiently fatiguing undertaking under the unclouded weather and over the unshaded downs that form the parade ground for the cadets. West Point is a military establishment containing some two hundred and fifty pupils; who are here educated for the army under the superintendence of experienced officers.*   The buildings, in which

* If the results answer to the means employed, the pupils of West Point ought to turn out accomplished scholars in

they reside and pursue their various studies, stand
upon a grassy knoll holding the top of the rocky

---

every branch of human learning, as well as ripe soldiers and
skilful engineers. Their course of education consists of
almost every study within the range of man's capacity; and
as the school discipline is unusually strict, their hours of
labour many, and of recreation very few, they should be able
to boast of many " wise men " among their number. However it is here, I imagine, as elsewhere; where studies are
pursued laboriously for a length of time, variety becomes a
necessary relief to the mental powers, and so far the multi-
plicity of objects of acquirement may be excused; but surely,
to combine in the education of one youth the elements of
half a dozen sciences, each one of which would wear out a
man's life in the full understanding of it, is not the best
system of instruction. However, 't is the one now univer-
sally adopted, and tends to give more smatterers in science
than scientific men to the world. The military part of
their education is, however, what the pupils of West Point
are most exercised in, and so far as one so ignorant of such
matters as myself can judge, I should imagine the system
adopted calculated to make expert artillerymen and engineers
of them. Their deportment, and the way they went through
their evolutions on the parade, did not appear to me very
steady — there was a want of correctness of carriage, generally, and of absolute precision cf movement, which one accustomed to the manœuvring of regular troops detects
immediately. There are several large pieces of ordnance
kept in the gun-room, some of which were taken from the
English; and I remarked a pretty little brass cannon, which
almost looked like a plaything, which bore the broad arrow
and the name of Saratoga.

bank of the river, and commanding a most enchanting view of its course. They are not particularly extensive; but commodious and well-or-
dered. I am told they have a good library; but
on reaching the dwelling of Mr. Cozzens, (proprietor of the hotel, which being at this season
shut, he received us most hospitably and courte-
ously in his own house,) I felt so weary, that I
thought it impossible I should stir again for the
whole day, and declined seeing it. I had walked
on the deck at an amazing pace, and without once
sitting down from eight o'clock till eleven; and I
think must nearly have killed Colonel ——, who
was my companion during this march. However,
upon finding that it wanted full an hour till dinner-
time, it was agreed that we should go up to the
fort, and we set off under the guidance of one of
Mr. Cozzens' servants, who had orders not to go
too fast with us. Before turning into the woods
that cover the foot of the mountain, we followed
a bit of road that overhung the river; and stealing
over its sleepy-looking waters, where shone like
stars the white sails of many a tiny skiff, came the
delicious notes of a bugle-horn. The height at
which we stood above the water prevented the ear
being satisfied with the complete subject of the
musician, but the sweet, broken tones that came

rising from the far down thickets that skirted the
river, had more harmony than a distinct and perfect
strain.   I stood entranced to listen — the whole
was like a dream of fairy-land : but presently our
guide struck into the woods, and the world became
screened from our sight.   I had thought that I
was tired, and could not stir, even to follow the
leisurely footsteps of our cicerone; but tangled
brake and woodland path, and rocky height, soon
roused my curiosity, and my legs following there-
with, I presently outstripped our party, guide and
all, and began pursuing my upward path ; through
close growing trees and shrubs, over pale, shining
ledges of granite, over which the trickling mountain
springs had taken their silvery course; through
swampy grounds, where the fallen leaves lay like
gems under the still pools that here and there
shone dimly in little hollow glens ; over the soft
starry moss that told where the moist earth retained
the freshening waters, over sharp, hard splinters
of rock, and rough masses of stone.   Alone, alone,
I was alone and happy, and went on my way rejoicing, climbing and climbing still, till the green
mound of thick turf, and ruined rampart of the
fort arrested my progress.   I coasted the broken
wall ; and lighting down on a broad, smooth table
of granite fringed with young cedar bushes, I look-

ed down, and for a moment my breath seemed to stop, the pulsation of my heart to cease — I was filled with awe. The beauty and wild sublimity of what I beheld seemed almost to crush my faculties, — I felt dizzy as though my senses were drowning, — I felt as though I had been carried into the immediate presence of God. Though I were to live a thousand years, I never can forget it. The first thing that I distinctly saw was the shadow of a large cloud, which rolled slowly down the side of a huge mountain, frowning over the height where I stood. The shadow moved down its steep sunny side, threw a deep blackness over the sparkling river, and then passed off and climbed the opposite mountain on the other shore, leaving the world in the full blaze of noon. I could have stretched out my arms, and shouted aloud — I could have fallen on my knees, and worshipped — I could have committed any extravagance that ecstasy could suggest. I stood filled with amazement and delight, till the footsteps and voices of my companions roused me. I darted away, unwilling to be interrupted. Colonel —— was following me, but I peremptorily forbade his doing so, and was clambering on alone, when the voice of our guide assuring me that the path I was pursuing was impassable, arrested my course. My

father beckoned to me from above not to pursue
my track; so I climbed through a break, which
the rocky walls of nature and the broken fortifica-
tions of art rendered tolerably difficult of access,
and running round the wall joined my father on
his high stand, where he was holding out his arms
to me. For two or three minutes we mingled exclamations of delight and surprise: he then led
me to the brink of the rampart; and looking down
the opposite angle of the wall to that which I was
previously coasting, I beheld the path I was then
following break suddenly off; on the edge of a pre-
cipice several hundred feet down into the valley:
it made me gulp to look at it. Presently I left
my father, and after going the complete round of
the ruins, found out for myself a grassy knoll commanding a full view of the scene, sufficiently far
from my party not to hear their voices, and screened
from seeing them by some beautiful young cedar
bushes; and here I lay down and cried most
abundantly, by which means I recovered my senses,
which else, I think, must have forsaken me. How
full of thoughts I was! Of God's great might, and
gracious goodness, of the beauty of this earth, of
the apparent nothingness of man when compared
with this huge inanimate creation, of his wondrous
value, for whose delight and use all these fair things

were created. I thought of my distant home; that handful of earth thrown upon the wide waters, whose genius has led the kingdoms of the world — whose children have become the possessors of this new hemisphere. I rejoiced to think that when England shall be, as all things must be, fallen into the devouring past, her language will still be spoken among these glorious hills, her name revered, her memory cherished, her fame preserved here, in this far world beyond the seas, this country of her children's adoption. Poor old mother! how she would remain amazed to see the huge earth and waters where her voice is heard, in the name of every spot where her descendants have rested the soles of their feet: this giant inheritance of her sons, poor, poor, old England!   *

*   *   *   *   *

Where are the poets of this land? Why such a world should bring forth men with minds and souls larger and stronger than any that ever dwelt in mortal flesh. Where are the poets of this land? They should be giants, too; Homers and Miltons, and Goethes and Dantes, and Shakspeares. Have these glorious scenes poured no inspirings into hearts worthy to behold and praise their beauty? Is there none to come here and worship among these hills and waters till his heart burns within

him, and the hymn of inspiration flows from his
lips, and rises to the sky? Is there not one among
the sons of such a soil to send forth its praises to
the universe, to throw new glory round the mountains, new beauty over the waves? Is inanimate
nature, alone, here " telling the glories of God?"
Oh, surely, surely, there will come a time when
this lovely land will be vocal with the sound of
song, when every close-locked valley and waving
wood, rifted rock and flowing stream, shall have
their praise. Yet 't is strange how marvellously
unpoetical these people are! How swallowed up
in life and its daily realities, wants, and cares!
How full of toil and thrift, and money-getting
labour! Even the heathen Dutch, among us the
very antipodes of all poetry, have found names
such as the Donder Berg for the hills, whilst the
Americans christen them Butter Hill, the Crows
Nest, and *such like*. Perhaps some hundred years
hence, when wealth has been amassed by individuals, and the face of society begins to grow
checkered, as in the old lands of Europe, when
the whole mass of population shall no longer go
running along the level road of toil and profit,
when inequalities of rank shall exist, and the rich
man shall be able to pay for the luxury of poetry,
and the poor man who makes verses no longer

be asked, " Why don't you cast up accounts?" when all this comes to pass, as *perhaps* some day it may, America will have poets. It seems strange to me that men, such as the early settlers in Massachussets, the Puritan founders of New England, the " Pilgrim Fathers," should not have had amongst them some men, or at least man, in whose mind the stern and enduring courage, the fervent, enthusiastic piety, the unbending love of liberty, which animated them all, become the inspiration to poetic thought, and the suggestion of poetical utterance. They should have had a Milton or a Klopstock amongst them. Yet, after all, they had excitement of another sort, and, moreover, the difficulties and dangers, and distresses of a fate of unparalleled hardship, to engross all the energies of their minds; and I am half inclined to believe that poetry is but a hothouse growth, and yet I don't know : I wish somebody would explain to me every thing in this world that I can't make out. *

* It might be a curious and interesting matter of research to determine under what combination of external circumstances the spirit of poetry flourishes most vigorously, and good poets have most abounded. The extremes of poverty and luxury seem alike inimical to its well-being; yet the latter far more so than the former, for most poets have been poor; some so poor, as to enrich the world, while they themselves received so little return from its favour as miser-

We came down from the mountain at about half-past one: our party had been joined by Colonel

---

ably to perish of want. Again, the level tenor of a life alike removed from want and superfluity should seem too devoid of interest or excitement to make a good poet. Long-lived competency is more favourable to the even temper of philosophy than the fiery nature of one who must know the storms of passion, and all the fiercer elements of which the acting and suffering soul of man is made. Again, it would be curious to know, if it might be ascertained, whether those men whose inspirations have been aided alone by the comtemplation of the inanimate beauties of nature, and the phenomena of their own minds and the minds and lives of their fellows, have been as great poets as those, who, besides these sources of inspiration, fed the power within them with the knowledge of great writers and poets of other countries and times. Another question, which it would be interesting to determine, would be, under what species of government poets have been most numerous, and most honoured. As our modern exploders of old fallacies have not yet made up their minds whether such a person as Homer ever lived, it is rather a vain labour of imagination to determine whether this great king of all poets flourished under a monarchy, or in a republic; certain it is, he sang of kings and princes in right lordly style : be that as it may, we have rather better authority for believing that the Greek dramatists, those masters, and sometime models, of their peculiar branch of the art, flourished under republican governments; but with them, I think, ends the list of republican poets of great and universal fame. Rome had no poets till she had emperors. Italy was, it is true, divided into so called republics during the golden age of her literature; but they were so in name alone, the spirit of equality had long departed from the soil,

——, Governor of the College, who very courte-
ously came toiling up to Fort Putnam, to pay his
compliments to us. I lingered far behind them,
returning; and, when they were out of sight,
turned back, and once more ascended the ruin, to
look my last of admiration and delight, and then
down, down, every step bringing me out of the
clouds, farther from heaven, and nearer this work
i' day world. I loitered, and loitered, looking back

---

and they were merely prouder and more arbitrary aristocra-
cies than have ever existed under any monarchy in the
world. If ever France can be said to have had a poetical
age, it was during the magnificent reign of Lewis the Four-
teenth, that pageant that prepared the bloodiest tragedy in
the pages of history. England offers the only exception
that I have advanced, namely, that the republican form of
government is inimical to poetry. For it was during the
short and shameful period of fanatical republicanism, which
blots her annals, that the glory and the might of Milton
rose upon the world; he is the only great poet who ever
flourished under a republic; and he was rather the poet of
heaven and hell, than of earth: his subjects are either bibli-
cal or mythological; and however his stern and just spirit
might advocate the cause of equality and universal freedom
in the more arid regions of political and theological contro-
versies, in his noblest and greatest capacity, he has sung of
angels and archangels, the starry hierarchy of heaven, where
some of the blessed wore a brighter glory than their fellows,
where some were inferior to other celestial powers, and
where God was King supreme, over all. In heaven, Milton
dreamt of no republics, nor in hell either.

at every step; but at last the hills were shut out
by a bend in the road, and I came into the house
to throw myself down on the floor, and sleep most
seriously for half an hour; at the end of which
time, we were called to dinner. In England, if
an innkeeper gives you a good dinner, and places
the first dish on the table himself, you pay him,
and he's obliged to you. Here, an innkeeper is a
gentleman, your equal, sits at his table with you,
you pay him, and are obliged to him besides.
'T is necessary therefore for a stranger, but especially an Englishman, to understand the fashions
of the land, else he may chance to mistake that
for an impertinent familiarity, which is in fact the
received custom of the country. Mr. Cozzens
very considerately gave us our dinner in a private
room, instead of seating us at an ordinary with
all the West Point Officers. Moreover, *gave* in
the literal sense, and a very good dinner it was.
He is himself a very intelligent, courteous person,
and, during the very short time that we were his
guests, showed us every possible attention and
civility. We had scarce finished our dinner, when
in rushed a waiter to tell us that the boat was in
sight. Away we trotted, trailing cloaks, and
shawls, any-how fashion, down the hill. The
steamer came puffing up the gorge between the

mountains, and in a moment we were bundled into the boat, hauled alongside, and landed on the deck; and presently the glorious highlands, all glowing in the rosy sunset, began to recede from us. Just as we were putting off from shore, a tiny skiff, with its graceful white sail glittering in the sun, turned the base of the opposite hill, evidently making to the point whence we embarked. I have since learned that it contained a messenger to us, from a gentleman bearing our name, and distantly connected with us, proprietor of some large iron works on the shore opposite West Point. However, our kinsman was too late, and we were already losing sight of West Point, when his boat reached the shore. Our progress homeward was, if any thing, more enchanting than our coming out had been, except for leaving all this loveliness. The sun went down in splendour, leaving the world robed in glorious beauty. The sky was one glowing geranium curtain, into which the dark hills rose like shadow-land, stretching beyond, and still beyond, till they grew like hazy outlines through a dazzling mist of gold. The glory faded; and a soft violet colour spread downwards to the horizon, where a faint range of clouds lay floating like scattered rose leaves. As the day fell, the volumes of smoke from our steam-boat chimneys became streams of fiery sparks, which glittered over the water with a strange unearthly effect. I sat on deck watching the world grow dark, till my father, afraid of the night air, bade me go down; and there, in spite of the chattering of a score of women, and the squalling of half as many children, I slept profoundly till we reached New York, at a quarter to seven.

Saturday, 17*th.*

After breakfast, wrote journal: while doing so, Mr. —— called to know if I held my mind in spite of the grey look of the morning. A wan sunbeam just then lighted on the earth, and I said I would go; for I thought by about twelve it probably would clear.   *   *

  *   *   *   *   *

  *   *   *   *   *

They called for me in the carriage at eleven; and afterwards we mounted our steeds in Warren Street to escape the crowd in Broadway. We rode down to the ferry. The creature, *on top* of which I sat, was the real *potatuppy* butcher's horse. However, it did not shake me, or pull my arms much, so I was content. As to a horse properly broken, either for man or woman, I have done looking for it in this land.   We went into the steam-boat on our horses.   The mist lay thick over the river; but the opposite shores had that grey distinctness of colour and outline that invariably foretells rain in England.   The wind blew bitterly keen and cold.   *   *   *

*   *   *   *   *.

Our riding party was Mr. ——, whom I like; Mrs. ——, whom I also like, in spite of her out-landish riding habiliments, a brother of his,   *

*   *   *   *   *

and a young —— in white hair and spectacles. The carriage held old Mr. ——, Miss ——, the youngest daughter, and that beautiful youngest boy of theirs, who is so like his handsome sister; also sundry baskets of cake, and bottles of cham-pagne.   After landing, we set off at a brisk canter to Weehawk.   None of these people know how to ride: they just go whatever pace their horse likes, sitting as backward as they can in the saddle, and tugging at the reins as hard as ever they can, to the infinite detriment of their own hands and their horses' mouths.   When we had reached the height, we dismounted and walked through the woods that crown the cliffs, which here rise to an eleva-tion of some hundred feet above the river.   Our path lay through tangled brakes, where the withered trees and fallen red leaves, the bright cedar bushes, and pale slabs of granite, formed a fine and harmonious contrast of colouring; the whole blending beautifully together under the grey light, that made it look like one of Ruysdael's pictures. Our walk terminated at a little rocky promontory, called the Devil's Pulpit, where, as legends say, Satan was wont to preach, loud enough to drown the sound of the Sabbath bells in New York. The Hudson, far below, lay leaden and sullen; the woods along the shores looked withered and wintry; a thick curtain of vapour shrouded all the distance: the effect of the whole was very sad and beautiful; and had I been by myself I should have enjoyed it very much. But I was in company, and, moreover, in company with two punsters, who uttered their atrocities without remorse in the midst of all that was most striking and melancholy in nature. When we mounted our horses again, Mrs. —— complained that hers pulled her wrists most dreadfully; and as they seemed none of the strongest, I exchanged steeds with her. The lady proprietress of the grounds over which we had been walking and riding invited us into the house, but being mounted I declined, and we set off for the pavilion. Just as we arrived there, it began to rain. Mercy on me and Mrs. ——! how our

arms will ache to-morrow! This worthy animal of
hers had a mouth a little worse than a donkey's.
Arrived at the pavilion, we dismounted, and swallowed sundry champagnes and lumps of plum
cake, which were singularly refreshing. We set
off again, and presently it began to pelt with rain.
We reached and crossed the ferry without getting
very wet. Arranged to ride on Wednesday, if
fine, and so home. Upon the whole, rather satisfied than otherwise with my expedition. Dressed
for dinner at once; went on with journal; Colonel —— called, and sat some time. After dinner,
embroidered till eight: teaed: — my father went
over to the theatre: I practised for two hours.

Sunday, 18*th.*

The muscles of my arms (for I have such un-
lady-like things) stand out like lumps of stone,
with the fine exercise they had yesterday. I wonder
how Mrs. ——'s shoulders and elbows feel. *

*   *   *   *   *

It rained so, we hackneyed to church. This is
twice Mr. —— has not been to church, which is
really very wrong, though it leaves us the pew
comfortably to ourselves. Dr. —— must be an
excellent good man — his sermons are every way

delightful; good sense, sound doctrine, and withal a most winning mildness and gentleness of manner. A benevolent good man, I am sure, he must be. Came home — copied snuff-box verses for my father; divided out my story of the Sisters into acts and scenes: began doing the same by the English tragedy; but in the midst took a fancy to make a story instead of a play of it — and so I will, I think. Dressed for dinner. At about half-past five Colonel —— and his Quaker wife came. She is a most delightful creature, with the sweetest expression of face imaginable. She reminded me several times of dear Mrs. ——. Her dress, too, the rich brown watered silk, made so plainly, recalled Mrs. —— to me very forcibly. We had a very comfortable dinner and evening. They went away at about half-past ten.

Monday, 19*th.*

After breakfast, wrote journal. Went out shopping and returning cards; called at Mrs. ——, and was let in. I like her; she is a nice person, with agreeable manners. Came home at about half-past two; put out things for the theatre; dined at three. After dinner, pottered about clothes till time to go to the theatre. The house was very good. My benefit — play, Much Ado about Nothing. I played very well. I am much improved in my comedy acting. Came home in a coach — it poured with rain. What a stupidday! The accounts of cholera in New Orleans are frightful; they have the yellow fever there too. Poor people! what an awful visitation!

Tuesday, 20th.

After breakfast, wrote journal. At twelve, went and called upon Mrs. ——: the day was bright, but bitter cold, with a keen piercing wind that half cut one in half, and was delicious. The servant denied Mrs. ——; but we had hardly turned from the door when both the ladies came rushing after us, with nothing on their heads and necks, and thin summer gowns on. They brought us into a room where there was a fire fit to roast an ox. No wonder the women here are delicate and subject to cold, and die of consumption. Here were these sitting absolutely in an oven, in clothes fit only for the hottest days in summer, instead of wrapping themselves up well, and trotting out, and warming their blood wholesomely with good hard exercise. The pretty Mrs. —— looks very sickly, and coughs terribly. Her beauty did not strike me so much to-day. I do not admire any body who looks as if a puff of wind would break them in half, or a drop of water soak them through. I greatly prefer her sister's looks, who certainly is not pretty, but tall and straight, and healthy-looking, and springy as a young thing ought to be. Was introduced to a most enchanting young Newfoundland dog, whom I greatly coveted. Settled to ride to-morrow if fine. Called at ——'s, also at a furrier's about cap, and came home. Found —— and —— with my father. What a very bad expression of face the former has; sneering and false — terrible! I looked at —— with much respect. I like his spirit, as it shines through his works, greatly. He was a pale, sickly-looking man, without any thing at all remarkable in the expression of his countenance. While they were here, Mr. —— called to settle about to-morrow. He is a nice person; sensible and civil, and civil in the right way. Arrangements were made for dear ——'s going, which I rejoiced in greatly. I do not like at all leaving her behind. When the folks were gone, put out things for the theatre. While doing so, Mr. —— and Mr. and Mrs. —— called. Great discoursing about horses and horsemanship. Dined at three. After dinner, put fur upon my habit. At half-past five, went to the theatre. House very good; play, Hunchback. By the by, Colonel —— called to-day, to entreat me to go and see his " Honour, the Recorder," who had sent me tickets of admission to the town hall, to see —— receive the freedom of the city. I could not go, because of our horseback expedition — this by the way. I played so-soish. —— was at the play; and at the end, somebody in the house exclaimed, " Three cheers for —— !" whereupon a mingled chorus of applause and hisses arose. The Vice-President looked rather silly, and acknowledged neither the one or the other. How well I remember the Duke of —— coming to the orchestra to see this play, the night before it was expected the Whigs would go out. I dare say he knew little enough what the Hunchback was about. I do not think the people noticed him, however; so the feeling of the pulse must have been unsatisfactory. Mr. —— said to Modus to-night in the play, speaking of me, " a change of linen will suffice for her." How absurd! we were all dying on the stage. Came home; supped: — looked at silks; chose a lovely rose-coloured one to line my Portia dress; with which good deed my day ended.

Wednesday, 21st.

Looked at the sun, and satisfied with his promise, went to bed again, and slept till half-past
eight. After breakfast, wrote to his honour, the
Recorder, an humble apology in true Old Bailey
style. Wrote journal, and began practising. Mrs.
—— called before I was out of my bed to tell us
that the ——'s were not going, but that either her
husband or her brother-in-law would be too glad
to go in the gig with D——. This, however, the
latter refused, not choosing, as she said, to make
any young man do the penance of keeping her
company on a party of pleasure. Dear good old
D——! I was vexed and provoked; but it could
not be helped. At eleven, —— came for me. I
found Mrs. —— in the carriage waiting for me.
We adjourned to Warren Street, where were assembled all the party. While we waited for our
horses, Neptune, the beautiful Newfoundland, was
admitted, and amused himself by prancing over
tables, and chairs, and sofas, to his own infinite
delight, and the visible benefit of the furniture.
Our steeds having arrived, we mounted and began
to progress. Myself, and Mrs. ——, her husband,
his brother, ——, and papa ——, Dr. ——,

Mrs. ——'s brother, and Mr. ——, nephew, I believe, of the Irish patriot, were the equestrians of the party. After, followed Mr. —— and Mrs. ——, all be-coated and be-furred, in the stanhope. After, followed the ammunition waggon, containing a negro servant, Neptune, and sundry baskets of champagne, cake, and cherry bounce. Away we rushed down Broadway, to the infinite edification of its gaping multitudes. Mr. —— had gotten me an enchanting horse that trotted like an angel. So in spite of Major ——'s awful denunciation of " disgusting," I had a delicious hard trot all through the streets, rising in my saddle like a lady, or rather, a gentleman. My habit seemed to excite considerable admiration and approbation, and indeed it was *great*. Crossed the Brooklyn ferry in the steam-boat, and safely landed on the opposite side. The whole army defiled; the stanhope taking the van, the horses forming the main body, and the provisions bringing up the rear. Our party separated constantly, as we progressed, into various groups, but I remained chiefly with Dr. ——, Mr. ——, and old Mr. ——. By the by, those ——'s are a charming family; for Mrs. —— sits straight in her saddle, and the Doctor settled, when we started, that when he had *despatched his patients*, he would call for D—— in the gig, and come down to meet us at the fort. Our ride thither was extremely agreeable: the day was clear, cold, and grey; a delightful day for riding. I trotted to my heart's content; and kept my blood warm, and my spirits like champagne, till we reached the fort, when, at sight of the Narrows, and the Sandy Hook light-house, they sank deep, deep down.　　＊

＊　　＊　　＊　　＊　　＊

＊　　＊　　＊　　＊　　＊

The sea lay grey and still, without a wave or scarce a ripple. A thousand light skiffs, of various shapes, lay upon the leaden waters. The sky was a fine heap of heavy purple clouds, from behind which the sun shot down his rays, which threw a melancholy wan lustre on the sea beneath them. 'T was a sad and beautiful scene. The colouring of the whole was gloomily harmonious; and the dark shores and grey expanse of water blended solemnly with the violet-coloured curtain of the heavens. We went over the fort. 'T is a fortification of no great size, or, I should think, strength; but its position, which commands the narrow entrance to the bay of New York, effectually checks the pass, and guards the watery defile that leads to the city of mammon. We looked at the guns and powder magazine, walked round the walls, and peeped into the officers' quarters, and then descended to seek where we might eat and be satisfied. Mrs. —— is a very nice creature: she looks the picture of good temper — never stands still a minute; and as we rode along to-day, when, fearing she might be cold, I asked her how she found herself, she replied, with perfect innocence and sincerity, " Oh, delightful !" which made us all scream. We knocked up the quarters of an old woman who kept a cottage, not exactly young love's humble shed, but good enough for our purpose. We got sundry logs of wood, and made a blazing fire; moreover, the baskets were opened, and presently we presented the interesting spectacle of a dozen people each with a lump of cake in one hand, and a champagne glass in the other. Mr. —— and Mrs. —— stuck to the cherry bounce, and, as we afterwards heard, drove home accordingly. Having discussed, we remounted, and set forwards home by another road; a very lovely one, all along the river side. Ere we had progressed long, we met D—— and Dr. —— in the gig. The nice good man had kept his word, and gone to fetch her. They had met Mr. ——'s equipage going cherry-bounce pace, it seems, two miles ahead of us. The men here are never happy unless they are going full speed. 'T is no wonder their horses are good for nothing : they would ruin

any horses that were good for any thing.* Such un-
skilful horsemanship I never saw : Going full tear;
crossing one another in every direction; knocking up against one another; splashing through
puddles because they have no hand over their
horses, and either overshooting their point, or being half thrown at every turn of the road for the
same reason. Came home full speed, and arrived
at half-past four, having ridden, I should think,
nearly twenty miles. Found Mrs. —— at home.
They pressed me very much to stay dinner with
them; but my father expected me, and I would
not. That worthy youth, ——, insisted upon my
accepting his beautiful large dog, Neptune, which
I did conditionally, in case Mr. —— should fail
me, which I think a very improbable case indeed.
They ordered the carriage, and Mr. —— persisted

* It is quite curious to observe how utterly unknown a
thing a *really* well broken horse is in this country. I have
just bought one who was highly approved and recommended
by several gentlemen considered here as learned in all these
matters; and of my own knowledge, I might hunt the Union
over and not find a better. As far as the make, and beauty,
and disposition of the animal goes, there is no fault to find;
but this *lady's horse* never had a woman on its back, had
never been ridden but with a snaffle bit, and until she came
into my possession, did not know how to canter with her
right foot. When the Americans say a horse is well broken,
they mean it is not wild.

in seeing me home in it, much to my annoyance, as 't was a very useless ceremony indeed. Did not dishabit, but dined *en amazone.*   *

*   *   *   *   *

Gave D—— her muff and tippet, which are exceedingly magnificent. After dinner, pottered about, and dressed at once. Played on the piano till nine, when we adjourned to ——'s. A complete "small party, my dear." Dr. —— was there, whom I was glad to see; also Mrs. ——; also Mr. and Miss ——; also that Mrs. ——, who is utter horror and perturbation of spirit to me; also ——; also ——; all our riding party, and a world besides. After a little time, dancing was proposed; and I stood up to waltz with Mr. ——, who observed that Dr. —— was gone, as he never chose to be present while waltzing was going on. I felt shocked to death that unconsciously I should have been instrumental in driving him away, and much surprised that those who knew his disapprobation of waltzing should have proposed it. However, he was gone, and did not return. Therefore I waltzed myself out of my conscientious remorse. Sang them Fanny Gray, and Ye Mariners of Spain. Danced sundry quadrilles; and, finally, what they called a Kentucky reel, — which is nothing more than Sir Roger de

Coverly turned Backwoodsman — and afterwards a " foursome reel." Played magic music; and, finally, at one o'clock, came home, having danced myself fairly off my legs.

Thursday, 22d.

It poured with rain all day. Dr. —— called, and gave me a sermon about waltzing. As it was perfectly good sense, to which I could reply nothing whatever in the shape of objection, I promised him never to waltz again, except with a woman, or my brother.   *   *
   *   *   *   *   *

After all, 't is not fitting that a man should put his arm round one's waist, whether one belongs to any one but one's self or not. 'Tis much against what I have always thought most sacred, — the dignity of a woman in her own eyes and those of others. I like Dr. —— most exceedingly. He spoke every way to my feelings of what was right, to-day. After saying that he felt convinced, from conversations which he had heard amongst men, that waltzing was immoral in its tendency, he added, " I am married, and have been in love, and cannot imagine any thing more destructive of the deep and devoted respect which love is calculated to excite in every honourable man's heart, not only for the individual object of his affections, but for her whole sex, than to see any and every impertinent coxcomb in a ball-room come up to her, and, without remorse or hesitation, clasp her waist, imprison her hand, and absolutely whirl her round in his arms." So spake the Doctor; and my sense of propriety and conviction of right bore testimony to the truth of his saying. So, farewell, sweet German waltz! — next to hock, the most intoxicating growth of the Rheinland. I shall never keep time to your pleasant measure again! — no matter; after all, any thing is better than to be lightly spoken of, and to deserve such mention. Mr. —— called, and sat some time with me. He is grown monstrously fat, and looks perfectly radiant. He brought with him a good-looking staring man of the name of ——. We dined at three. After dinner, received a pretty anonymous nosegay, with sundry very flattering doggrel. The play was the Stranger. It poured cats and dogs, and the streets were all grey pudding. I did not expect to see six people in the house; instead of which, 'twas crowded : a satisfactory proof of our attraction.

Friday, 23d.

At eleven, went to rehearsal — Isabella. I have forgotten all about it. They all read their parts; came home; began to practise. The two Mrs. —— called. I like them mainly, Mrs. —— particularly. While they were here, Mr. —— and a man called; they stayed but a minute. By and by, in walked Mr. and Mrs. ——; whereupon the —— departed.   *   *   *

*   *   *   *   *

*   *   *   *   *

While they were here, received from —— the beautiful annual he has bought for me, which is, indeed, most beautiful; and with it, literally a copy of verses, which are *not so bad neither* — only think of that ! ! ! The engravings are from things of Stanfield's, taken on the Rhine; and made my heart ache to be once more in Europe, in the old land where fairy tales are told; in the old feudal world, where every rock, and valley, and stream, are haunted with imaginings wild and beautiful : the hallowed ground of legend history; the dream-land of fancy and of poetry. Put out things for the theatre : dined at three. Colonel —— called : he brought news of the arrival of a

Liverpool packet, and prophesied letters to me.
Went to the theatre. Play, Hunchback — house
very fine again. Just as I was dressing for the
second act, three letters were brought into my
room. * * * *
* * * * *
* * * * *

I was so much overset by them, that, with the
strange faculty I have of pouring one feeling into
another, I cried so bitterly in the parting scene
with Clifford, that I could scarcely utter the words
of my part. * * *
* * * * *
* * * * *

Saturday, 24th.

Our riding expedition having been put off, the
day was beautifully bright and clear. Sat stitching and pottering an infinity. My feet got so
perished that I didn't know what to do. Wrote
journal; practised for an hour; Mr. —— called.
When he was gone, went out with my father.
Called at ——'s to order home my gown for dinner-time. Left a card at Mrs. ——'s, and then
marched down to the tailor's to upbraid him about

my waistcoat, which is infamously ill made.* Coming home, met that very odious Mr. ———, who is
the perfection of genteel vulgarity. He walked
home with us. Dressed for dinner. Mme. ———
did not send my gown home in time: abominable
sempstress! so put on my blue and looked rather
dowdy. Found sundry that we knew: Colonel
———; Mr. ———; my favourite aversion, Mr.
———; that signal fool, Mr. ———; Miss ———, who
looked like a hair-dresser's wax block; a Miss ———,
with lovely feet, and a terrified Bacchante-looking
head, *cum multis aliis.* I sat by one Mr. ———,
who talked without end, and cleverly enough: indeed, it was rather clever to talk so wonderfully
fast and much. After dinner, the party became

---

* The various censures which English travellers have bestowed upon various things in this country are constantly,
both in private conversation and the public prints, attributed
to *English jealousy.* I confess I have been amused at the
charge, and can only sincerely hope I may not draw down so
awful an accusation on myself, when I declare, that, during a
three years' residence in America, almost every article, of
every description, which I have had made, has been ill made,
and obliged to undergo manifold alterations. I don't pre-
tend to account for the fact, for fear the obvious reasons
might appear to find their source in that very small jealousy
of which England is guilty towards this country, in the person of her journal-scribbling travellers; but to the fact there
is and can be no denial.

much larger : Dr. ——, Mr. ——, the —— (all
but ——), that entire self-satisfaction, Mr. ——,
Mr. ——, and the knight of the rueful countenance;
three singing men, ycleped ——; and a shoal besides. One of the Mr. —— and Miss —— sang
the duet in the Didone, that dear —— and ——
used to sing so lovelily. They both had good
voices, but the style is but so-soish. Presently,
three men sang that sea glee that I remember
Lord and Lady —— teaching me at ——. What
a strange faculty of our nature this is, this leading
back of our minds to the past, through the agency
of our senses, acted upon by present influences,
the renewing life, the magical summoning up of
dead time from its grave, with the very place and
circumstance it wore. Wondrous riddle ! what
—— what are we, that are so curiously made ? By
and by dancing was proposed, and I was much
entreated and implored to change my determination about waltzing; but I was inexorable, and
waltzed only with the ladies, who one and all dance
extremely well. Mrs. —— looked lovely to-night.
Dr. —— says very true, she has a thorough-bred
look, which reminds me a little of our noble English ladies. He says she is like Lady ——. I
think she is prettier: she certainly looks like a
gem. We danced a Kentucky reel, and sundry

quadrilles. That long *ens*, Mr. ——, was tipsy, and went slithering about in a way to kill one; and Mr. —— was sitting slyly in the corner, pretending to talk to D——, but in fact dying with laughter at poor ——, who meandered about the room to the infinite dismay and confusion of the whole dance. Vain were the vigorous exertions of his partner, who pulled him this way and that, and pushed him hither and thither, to all which the unresisting creature submitted incorrigibly. Remained dancing till half-past twelve, in fact, Sunday morning, and then came home. They made me sing, which I did abominably. On my return home, found my black satin gown; every atom of which will have to be unpicked — pleasant! The trades-people here are really terrible; they can do nothing, and will take no pains to do any thing: 't is a handsome gown spoilt.*

* When you carry your complaint of careless work, or want of punctuality, to the trades-people whom you employ here, the unfortunate principals really excite your sympathy by their helpless situation with regard to the free republicans whom they employ, and who, with the utter comtempt of subordination which the cheapness of living, and the spirit of licence (not liberty) produce among the lower classes here, come when they please, depart when they like, work when they choose, and if you remonstrate, take themselves off to new masters, secure of employment in your

Sunday, 25th.

My dear father's birth-day! also, by the by, a grand occasion here — the anniversary of the evacuation of the island by the British troops, which circumstance the worthy burghers have celebrated ever since with due devotion and thankfulness. Went to church: Dr. —— did not preach, which was a disappointment to me. The music was exquisite; and there was a beautiful graceful willow branch, with its long delicate fibres and golden leaves, waving against the blue sky and the

---

neighbour's house, if your mode of employing them displeases them. Manifold are the lamentations I have heard, of " Oh, ma'am, this is not like the old country; we can't get journeymen to work here, ma'am; we're obliged to do just as our workmen please, ma'am." One poor French dress-maker appeared to me on the verge of distraction, from the utter impossibility of keeping in any order a tribe of sewing girls, whom she seemed to pay on purpose that they might drive her crazy; and my shoemaker assured me the other day, with a most woful face, that it was election week, and that if I was as *suffering* for shoes as a lady could be, I could not have mine till the political cobblers in his employ had settled the " business of the nation " to their satisfaction. Patience is the only remedy. Whoever lives here, that has ever lived elsewhere, should come provided with it.

church window, that seemed to me like a magical branch in a fairy tale. It struck me as strange to-day, as I looked from the crowded gloomy church to the bright unbounded sky, to think that we call the one the house of God; to be sure, we have other authority for calling the blue heavens his throne; and oh, how glorious they did look! The day was bright, but bitter cold. Coming out of church, saw all our last night's party. On my return home, found a perfect levee; Dr. ——, Mr. ——, Mr. ——, Mr. ——, Mr. ——, a whole regiment. When they were all gone, wrote journal: having finished that and my lunch, set out with my father to *fetch a walk;* which we did to the tune of near six miles, through all the outskirts of the town, an exceedingly low-life ramble indeed — during which we came across a man who was preaching in the street. He had not a very large assembly round him, and we stood in the crowd to hear him. By his own account, he had been imprisoned before for a similar proceeding, and he was denouncing, most vehemently, signal judgments on the blind and wicked corporation who had so stopped the work of righteousness. The man's face was a very fine one, remarkably intelligent and handsome: he was cleanly and well dressed, and had altogether a respectable

appearance. When we came home, it was past
four. Dressed for dinner. My father dined with
Mr. ——; so D—— and I had a *tête-à-tête* dinner.
After which, played on the piano for some time;
after which, began letter to H——; after which,
wrote journal.   *   *   *

  *   *   *   *   *

  *   *   *   *   *

                              Monday, 26th.

Yesterday was evacuation day; but as yesterday
was the Lord's day also, the American militia army
postponed their yearly exhibition, and, instead of
rushing about the streets in token of their thankfulness at the departure of the British, they quietly
went to church, and praised God for that same.
To-day, however, we have had firing of pop-guns,
waving of star-spangled banners (some of them
rather the worse for wear), infantry marching
through the streets, cavalry (oh, Lord, what delicious objects they were!) and artillery prancing
along them, to the infinite ecstasy and peril of a
dense mob. Went to rehearsal at half-past ten.
Was detained full ten minutes on the way thither,
by the defiling of troops, who were progressing
down Broadway. After rehearsal, came home —

put out things for the theatre. Mr. —— called : while he was here, spent a delightful half hour at the window, which, overlooking the park, commanded a full view of the magnanimous military marshalled there. O, pomp and circumstance of glorious war! They were certainly not quite so bad as Falstaff's men, of ragged memory; for, for aught I know to the contrary, they perhaps *all* of them had shirts to their backs. But some had gloves, and some had none ; some carried their guns one way, and some another ; some had caps of one fashion, and some of another; some had no caps at all, but " shocking bad hats," with feathers in them.*

* This description may amaze sundry narrow-minded and prejudiced dwellers in those unhappy countries where standing armies are among the standing abuses, and the miserable stipendiaries of hoary tyrannies go about wearing the livery of their trade with a slavish unanimity becoming alone to hirelings, and salaried butchers base. But whoever should imagine that the members of an enlightened and free republic must, because they condescend to become soldiers, for the pure love of their country, behave as soldiers also, would draw foolish conclusions. Discipline, order, a peculiar carriage, a particular dress, obedience to superiors, and observance of rules, these, indeed, may all be the attributes of such miserable creatures as are content to receive wages for their blood. But for free Americans ! why should they not walk crooked, in the defence of their country, if they don't like to walk straight ? why should they not carry their guns on their shoulders instead of upright, if they please ?

The infantry were, however, comparatively respectable troops. They did not march many degrees out of the straight line, or stoop *too much*, or turn their heads round *too often*. Mr. ——— remarked, that militia were seldom more steady and orderly in their appearance. But the cavalry! oh, the cavalry! what gems without price they were! Apparently extremely frightened at the shambling *tituppy* chargers upon whose backs they clung, straggling in all directions, putting the admiring crowd in fear of their lives, and proving beyond a doubt how formidable they must appear to the enemy, when, with the most peaceable intentions in the world, they thus jeopardied the safety of their enthusiastic fellow-citizens. Bold would have been the man who did not edge backwards into the crowd, as a flock of these worthies a-horseback came down the street — some trotting, some galloping, some racking, some ambling; each and all " witching the world with wondrous horsemanship." If any thing ever might

---

and why, since they chose to defend their lives and liberties by becoming volunteers, should they not stick any feathers, of any colours that they like in their caps — black, white, or green ? Is the noble occupation of war incompatible with the still nobler possession of freedom ? Heaven forbid ! and long live the American militia to prove their entire compatibility.

be properly called wondrous, they, their riders
and accoutrements, deserve the title. Some wore
boots, and some wore shoes, and one independent
hero had got on grey stockings and *slippers!* Some
had bright yellow feathers, and some red and
black feathers! I remembered, particularly, a
doctor, in a black suit, Hessian boots, a cocked
hat, and bright yellow gauntlets; another fellow
was dressed in the costume of one of the Der
Freyschutz's corps: it looked for all the world like
a *fancy* parade. The officers fulfilled completely
my idea of Macheath's company of gentlemen of
the road; only, I strongly suspect the latter would
have been heartily ashamed of the unhappy hacks
the evacuation heroes had gotten up upon. The
parade terminated with a full half hour's *feu de
joie.*† * * * *

† The militia has fallen into disrepute of late in New
York and Philadelphia. Trainings and parades take too
much of the precious time, whose minutes are cents, and
hours dollars. The only instance of humour, national or
individual, which I have witnessed since my abode in this
country, was a sham parade got up in mimicry of the real
one here described. In this grotesque procession, every
man was dressed in the most absurd costume he could
devise: banners with the most ludicrous inscriptions, wooden
swords of gigantic dimensions, and children's twopenny guns
were some of their paraphernalia; and, in the absurd and

* * * * *
* * * * *

The bands of these worthies were worthy of them ; half a dozen fifers and drummers playing old English jig tunes. In spite of the folly and injustice of such a comparison, I could not keep out of my head the last soldiers I had seen, those fine tall fellows, the grenadier guards, that used to delight us of a Sunday morning in St. James's Park, and their exquisite band, and dandy-looking officers. Those *looked* like soldiers, whatever they may fight like ; and allowing these excellent good folks to be very lions, look you, I can only say their appearance approached the sublime, by as near as the French critic assures us the extreme

---

monstrous objects the men had made of themselves, with false whiskers, beards, and noses, I recognised some of the broad, coarse, powerful humour of the lower orders in the old country. But it is the *only* symptom of such a spirit which I have met with. The absolute absence of imagination, of course, is also the absolute absence of humour. An American can no more understand a fanciful jest than a poetical idea; and in society and conversation, the strictest matter of fact prevails : for any thing departing from it, though but an inch, either towards the sublime or the ridiculous, becomes immediately incomprehensible to your auditors, who will stare at your enthusiasm, and sincerely ask you the meaning of your jest.

of the ridiculous does. Dined at three; —— and —— called after dinner. My father went with Mr. —— to Tammany Hall*, where there was a grand democratic dinner, in honour of the triumph of the Jackson party, the mob men here. I sat writing to —— till time to go to the theatre. The play was Isabella; the house crammed; a regular holyday audience—shrieking, shouting, laughing, and rowing, like one of our own Christmas audiences. I acted like a wretch. My dresses looked very handsome, particularly my marriage dress; but my muslin bed-gown was so long that I set my feet through it the very first thing; and those *animaux bêtes*, who dragged me off, tore a beautiful point lace veil I had on to tatters, a thing that cost three guineas, if a farthing! My father received a most amusing letter this morning from Lord ——, asking us to come over to Jamaica and act, offering us quarters in his house, and plenty of volunteer actors (did he include himself, I wonder?) to make up a company, if we will come. I should like it very well: to pass the winter in that nice warm climate would be delightful, and I dare say we should find our stay

---

* A place devoted to political meetings, chiefly, however, I believe, those termed here " democratic."

there amusing and agreeable enough. I wish we
could do it.

Tuesday, 27th.

After breakfast, Colonel —— called. Put out
things for to-night. At half-past twelve, went out
with my father and Colonel ——. Called upon
his honour, the Recorder, but he was in court,
and not to be seen. Walked down to the Battery.
The day was most lovely, like an early day in
June in England : my merino gown was intolerable, and I was obliged to take a parasol with me,
the sun was so powerful. The Battery was, as
usual, totally deserted, though the sky, and shores,
and beautiful bright bay, were smiling in perfect
loveliness. A delicious fresh breeze came wandering over the wide estuary; and graceful boats,
with their full sails glittering in the sun, glided to
and fro, swift and strong, over the smooth waters,
like summer clouds across the blue heavens — as
silently, as rapidly, as tracklessly.†   *   *

† It is the property of perfection alone to rivet the admiration of absolute ignorance ; whence I conclude that the
river craft, hovering from morning till night along the waters
that surround New York, must be the most beautiful in the
world. Their lightness, grace, swiftness, and strength, ap-

*　　　*　　　*　　　*　　　*

*　　　*　　　*　　　*　　　*

Came home at half-past one. Found a card from Mrs. ———. I'm sorry I didn't see her. ——— called, with one Mr. ———, kinsman to the authoress.　*　　*　　*　　*

　*　　　*　　　*　　　*　　　*

　　*　　　*　　　*　　　*　　　*

While they were here, Mrs. ——— called to settle about to-morrow's ride. Mr. and Mrs. ——— arriving, the rest departed. We dined at three. After dinner, came to my own room; wrote journal; went on with letter to ———. At half-past five, went to the theatre. Play, the Gamester; my father's benefit; the house was very good. I played pretty well. Mr. ——— thoroughly bothered me, by standing six yards behind me: what a complete stroller's trick that is. So we are to act on Saturday. If I can go to the opera, all the same, I sha'n't mind so much; but I will be in most horrible dudgeon if it prevents that, for I want to hear this new prima donna. Mr. ——— was behind the scenes, and ——— *wrapt*, in his usual seat: he's a delightful bit of audience.

---

pear to me unequalled. Such beautiful vessels I never saw; more beautiful ones I cannot imagine.

Received a bill of the intended performances for Thursday, Mr. ——'s benefit; and such another farce as the whole thing is I never heard of; as Mr. —— says, "the benefit of humbug," indeed.

* * * * *

* * * * *

Came home. While we were at supper, my father showed me a note he had received from ——, which, to use a most admirable vulgarism, struck me all of a heap. A sort of threatening letter, desiring him, as he valued his interest, to come forward and offer to act Charles the Second for the said Mr. ——'s benefit, having already agreed to act in one piece, for said Mr. ——'s benefit. "O monstrous! monstrous! most unnatural!" What a vulgar wretch the man must be!

Wednesday, 28th.

Mary ——'s wedding day! Poor lassie! I looked at the bright morning sun with pleasure for her sake. After breakfast, sat reading the poems of Willis, a young man, whose works, young as they evidently are, would have won him some consideration in any but such a thorough work-day world as this. I cried a good deal over some of this man's verses.

I thought some of them beautiful; and 't is the property of beauty to stir the wells of my soul sadly, rather than cast sunshine over them. I think all things are sad. 'T is sad to hear sweet music; 't is sad to read fine poetry; 't is sad to look upon the beautiful face of a fair woman; 't is sad to behold the unclouded glory of a summer's sky. There is a deep and lingering tone in the harmony of all beauty that resounds in our souls with too full and solemn a vibration for pleasure alone. In fact, *intensity*, even of joy and delight, is in itself serious; 't is impossible to be fulfilled with emotion of any sort and not feel as though we were within the shadow of a cloud.* I remember when first I recited Juliet to my mother, she said I spoke the balcony scene almost sadly. Was not such deep, deep love too strong, too passionate, too pervading, to be uttered with the light laughing voice of pleasure? Was not that love, even in its fulness of joy, sad—awful? However, perhaps, I do but see through my own medium, and fancy it the universal one. My eyes are dark, and most things look darkly through

* In Canova's group of Cupid and Psyche, the young god is smiling like a god; but the eager parted lips with which Psyche is seeking his, wear no such expression — you might fancy they trembled, but they certainly do not smile.

them. At about twelve o'clock Mrs. —— called for me; and, escorted by her husband and Mr. ——, we rode forth to visit the island. We went to a pretty cottage belonging to Mr. ——'s father-in-law, Dr. ——. The day was still and grey — a pleasant day; there was no sunshine, but neither were there any dark shadows. My horse had been ill ridden by somebody or another, and was mighty disagreeable. Our ride was pleasant enough : there was not much variety in the country we passed through. Masses of granite and greenish basalt, wild underwood, and vivid bright-looking cedar bushes. The Hudson lay leaden and sullen under the wings of the restless wind. We stood to hear the delicious music of the water plashing against the rocky shore, which is the pleasantest sound in all the world. We then rode to a place ycleped Hell-gate*, from a dangerous current in the East river, where ships have been lost — and home through the mellow sunlight of a warm autumnal afternoon. Came in at a little past four.

* The ladies of New York, and all lady-like people there, have agreed to call this eddy *Hurl*-gate. The superior propriety of this name is not to be questioned; for hell is a shocking bad word, no doubt: but being infinitely more appropriate to the place and its qualities, I have ventured to mention it.

Devoured sundry puddings and pies; put out clothes for the evening; dined at five. My father dined at ———'s: I've an especial fancy for that man. After dinner, sat making blonde tippet, and strumming on the piano till eight. Drank tea, dressed, and off to Mrs. ———'s "small party, my dear."

         *   *   *   *

   *   *   *   *   *

   *   *   *   *   *

The people here have no conscience about the questions they ask; and, as I have one in answering, and always give them "the truth, the whole truth, and nothing but the truth," it follows that nothing can be more disagreeable than their queries, except my replies. Mr. ——— was there; I like him: he has something in him, and is not vulgar or impertinent. Was introduced to a very handsome French creole woman*, whom I liked: she reminded me of my mother, and her son bore

---

* The ladies here have an extreme aversion to being called *women*, I don't exactly understand why. Their idea is, that that term designates only the lower or less refined classes of female human-kind. This is a mistake which I wonder they should fall into; for in all countries in the world, queens, duchesses, and countesses, are called women; but in this one alone, washerwomen, sempstresses, and housemaids are entitled *ladies;* so that, in fact, here woman is by far the more desirable appellation of the two.

a striking resemblance to dear ——. We stood
up to dance a couple of quadrilles; but as they
had not one distinct idea of what the figures were,
the whole was a mess of running about, explain-
ing, jostling, and awkward blundering.*   I took
greatly to the governess of the family, a German
woman, with a right German face, a nice person,
with quiet simple manners.   The women's voices
here distract me; so loud, so rapid, and with
such a twang! What a pity! for they are, almost
without an exception, lovely-looking creatures,
with an air of refinement in their appearance,
which would be very attractive, but for their style
of dress, and those said tremendous shrill loud

---

* The established succession of figures which form the
one French quadrille, in executing which the ball-rooms of
Paris and London have spent so many satisfactory hours,
ever since it was invented, by no means satisfies the Americans.   At the close of almost every quadrille, a *fancy* figure
is danced, which, depending entirely upon the directions of
the leader of the band, is a very curious medley of all the
rest.   The company not being gifted with second sight, and
of course not knowing at every step what next they may be
called upon to do, go fearfully sliding along, looking at each
other, asking, " how does it go on ?" some *en avant deuxing*,
while others are starting off *en promenade*, the whole being
a complete confusion of purpose and execution.   The common French figure, the Trénis, is very seldom danced at all,
— they do not appear to know it.

voices.* Came home at twelve o'clock. My favourite aversion, Mrs. ——, was there.

* This terrible nuisance has often made me wish for that "still small voice," which has become the universal tone of good society in England, and which, however inconvenient sometimes from its utter inaudibility, at least did not send one to bed with one's ears ringing and one's head splitting. I was in a society of about twelve ladies, the other evening, and the *uproar* was so excessive that I felt my eyebrows contracting from a sense of perfect bewilderment, occasioned by the noise all round me, and more than once was obliged to request the person with whom I was conversing to stop till the *noise* had subsided a little, that I might be able to distinguish what he was saying to me. Were the women here large and masculine in their appearance, this defect would appear less strange, though not less disagreeable; but they are singularly delicate and feminine in their style of beauty; and the noise they make strikes one with surprise as something monstrous and unnatural — like mice roaring. They frequently talk four or five at a time, and directly across each other; neither of which proceedings is exactly according to my ideas of good breeding.

END OF THE FIRST VOLUME.

For EU product safety concerns, contact us at Calle de José Abascal, 56–1°, 28003 Madrid, Spain or eugpsr@cambridge.org.